ICSE 10

12 + 1 SAMPLE PAPERS

MOHIT TRIPATHI

EDUCATOR

B.Sc. (Maths), MCA, GNIIT

BOARD SAMPLE PAPER WITH SOLUTION & ANALYSIS BASED ON LATEST CIRCULAR ISSUED IN JULY FOR 2022-23 EXAM

Title : ICSE Class 10 Computer Application

Author Name : Mr. Mohit Tripathi

Published By : EduGorilla Community Pvt. Ltd.

Publishers Address : Sector-12/651, First Floor Opp. Arvindo Park, Near Jama Masjid, Indira Nagar, Lucknow, Uttar Pradesh-226016, India

Copyright

ISBN: 9789355564924

+91-63932 16806, +91-78000 04200
book@edugorilla.com
www.edugorilla.com

Disclaimer

Created & Compiled by EduGorilla Publication

Printed by EduGorilla Community Pvt. Ltd.

ICSE X COMPUTER

MIND MAP

SOLVED SAMPLE TEST PAPER

UNSOLVED SAMPLE TEST PAPER

PREVIOUS YEAR PAPER

MOST EXPECTED QUESTION PAPER

COMPUTER APPLICATIONS (86)

CLASS X

There will be **one** written paper of **two hours** duration carrying **100 marks** and Internal Assessment of **100 marks**.

THEORY – 100 Marks

Revision of Class IX Syllabus

(i) Introduction to Object Oriented Programming concepts, (ii) Elementary Concept of Objects and Classes, (iii) Values and Data types, (iv) Operators in Java, (v) Input in Java, (vi) Mathematical Library Methods, (vii) Conditional constructs in Java, (viii) Iterative constructs in Java, (ix) Nested for loops.

Class as the Basis of all Computation

Objects and Classes

Objects encapsulate state and behaviour – numerous examples; member variables; attributes or features. Variables define state; member methods; Operations/methods/messages/ methods define behaviour.

Classes as abstractions for sets of objects; class as an object factory; primitive data types, composite data types. Variable declarations for both types; difference between the two types. Objects as instances of a class. Consider real life examples for explaining the concept of class and object.

User - defined Methods

Need of methods, syntax of methods, forms of methods, method definition, method calling, method overloading, declaration of methods,

Ways to define a method, ways to invoke the methods – call by value [with programs] and call by reference [only definition with an example], Object creation - invoking the methods with respect to use of multiple methods with different names to implement modular programming, using data members and member methods, Actual parameters and formal parameters, Declaration of methods - static and non-static, method prototype / signature, - Pure and impure methods, - pass by value [with programs] and pass by reference [only definition with an example], Returning values from the methods , use of multiple methods and more than one method with the same name (polymorphism - method overloading).

Constructors

Definition of Constructor, characteristics, types of constructors, use of constructors, constructor overloading.

Default constructor, parameterized constructor, constructor overloading., Difference between constructor and method.

Library classes

Introduction to wrapper classes, methods of wrapper class and their usage with respect to numeric and character data types. Autoboxing and Unboxing in wrapper classes.

Class as a composite type, distinction between primitive data type and composite data type or class types. Class may be considered as a new data type created by the user, that has its own functionality. The distinction between primitive and composite types should be discussed through examples. Show how classes allow user defined types in programs. All primitive types have corresponding class wrappers. Introduce Autoboxing and Unboxing with their definition and simple examples.

The following methods are to be covered:

int parseInt(String s), long parseLong(String s), float parseFloat(String s), double parseDouble(String s), boolean isDigit(char ch), boolean isLetter(char ch), boolean isLetterOrDigit(char ch), boolean isLowerCase(char ch), boolean isUpperCase(char ch), boolean isWhitespace(char ch), char toLowerCase (char ch) char toUpperCase(char ch)

Encapsulation

Access specifiers and its scope and visibility. Access specifiers – private, protected and public. Visibility rules for private, protected and public access specifiers. Scope of variables, class variables, instance variables, argument variables, local variables.

Arrays

Definition of an array, declaration, initialization and accepting data of single dimensional array, accessing the elements of single dimensional array.

Arrays and their uses, sorting technique - bubble sort; Search techniques – linear search and binary search, Array as a composite type, length statement to find the size of the array (sorting and searching techniques using single dimensional array only).

String handling

String class, methods of String class, implementation of String class methods, String array

The following String class methods are to be covered:

String trim ()

String toLowerCase() String toUpperCase() int length( ) char charAt (int n) int indexOf(char ch) int lastIndexOf(char ch) String concat(String str) boolean equals (String str) boolean equalsIgnoreCase(String str) int compareTo(String str) int compareToIgnoreCase(String str)

String replace (char oldChar,char newChar) String substring (int beginIndex) String substring (int beginIndex, int endIndex) boolean startsWith(String str) boolean endsWith(String str)

String valueOf(all types)

Outputs based on all the above methods; Programs based on the above methods, extracting and modifying characters of a string, alphabetical order of the strings in an array [Bubble sort technique], searching for a string in a string array using linear search technique. SIMPLE Programs based on extraction of characters.

NOTE: PROGRAMS BASED ON EXTRACTION OF WORDS FROM A SENTENCE ARE NOT INCLUDED.

INTERNAL ASSESSMENT - 100 Marks

This segment of the syllabus is totally practical oriented. The accent is on acquiring basic programming skills quickly and efficiently.

Programming Assignments (Class X)

The students should complete a minimum of 20 laboratory assignments during the whole year to reinforce the concepts studied in class.

Suggested list of Assignments:

The laboratory assignments will form the bulk of the course. Good assignments should have problems which require design, implementation and testing. They should also embody one or more concepts that have been discussed in the theory class. A significant proportion of the time has to be spent in the laboratory. Computing can only be learnt by doing.

The teacher-in-charge should maintain a record of all the assignments done by the student throughout the year and give it due credit at the time of cumulative evaluation at the end of the year.

Some sample problems are given below as examples. The problems are of varying levels of difficulty:

(i) User defined methods

- **(a)** Programs depicting the concept of pure, impure, static, non- static methods.
- **(b)** Programs based on overloaded methods.
- **(c)** Programs involving data members, member methods invoking the methods with respect to the object created.

(ii) Constructors

- **(a)** Programs based on different types of constructors mentioned in the scope of the syllabus.
- **(b)** Programs / outputs based on constructor overloading.

(iii) Library classes

- **(a)** Outputs based on all the methods mentioned in the scope of the syllabus.
- **(b)** Programs to check whether a given character is an uppercase/ lowercase / digit etc.

(iv) Encapsulation

Questions based on identifying the different variables like local, instance, arguments, private, public, class variable etc.

(v) Arrays

- **(a)** Programs based on accessing the elements of an array.
- **(b)** Programs based on sort techniques mentioned in the scope of the syllabus.
- **(c)** Programs based on search techniques mentioned in the scope of the syllabus.

(vi) String handling

- **(a)** Outputs based on all the string methods mentioned in the scope of the syllabus.
- **(b)** Programs based on extracting the characters from a given string and manipulating the same.
- **(c)** Palindrome string, pig Latin, alphabetical order of characters, etc.

Important: This list is indicative only. Teachers and students should use their imagination to create innovative and original assignments.

EVALUATION

The teacher-in-charge shall evaluate all the assignments done by the student throughout the year [both written and practical work]. He/she shall ensure that most of the components of the syllabus have been used appropriately in the assignments. Assignments should be with appropriate list of variables and comment statements. The student has to mention the output of the programs.

Proposed Guidelines for Marking

The teacher should use the criteria below to judge the internal work done. Basically, four criteria are being suggested: class design, coding and documentation, variable description and execution or output. The actual grading will be done by the teacher based on his/her judgment. However, one possible way: divide the outcome for each criterion into one of 4 groups: excellent, good, fair/acceptable, poor/unacceptable, then use numeric values for each grade and add to get the total.

Class design:

Has a suitable class (or classes) been used?

Are all attributes with the right kinds of types present? Is encapsulation properly done? Is the interface properly designed

Coding and documentation:

Is the coding done properly? (Choice of names, no unconditional jumps, proper organization of conditions, proper choice of loops, error handling, code layout) Is the documentation complete and readable? (class documentation, variable documentation, method documentation, constraints, known bugs - if any).

Variable description:

Format for variable description:

Name of the Variable	Data Type	Purpose/description

Execution or Output:

Does the program run on all sample input correctly?

Evaluation of practical work will be done as follows:

Subject Teacher(Internal Examiner)		50 marks
External Examiner		50 marks

Criteria (Total- 50 marks)	Class design (10 marks)	Variable description (10 marks)	Coding and Documentation (10 marks)	Execution OR Output (20 marks)
Excellent	10	10	10	20
Good	8	8	8	16
Fair	6	6	6	12
Poor	4	4	4	8

An External Examiner shall be nominated by the Head of the School and may be a teacher from the faculty, but not teaching the subject in the relevant section/class. For example, A teacher of Computer Science of class VIII may be deputed to be the External Examiner for class X.

The total marks obtained out of 100 are to be sent to the Council by the Head of the school. The Head of the school will be responsible for the online entry of marks on the Council's CAREERS portal by the due date.

EQUIPMENT

There should be enough computer systems to provide for a teaching schedule where at least three-fourth of a time available is used for programming and assignments/practical work. The course shall require at least 4 periods of about 40 minutes duration per week. In one week, out of 4 periods the time should be divided as follows:

- 2 periods – Lecture cum demonstration by the Instructor.
- 2 periods – Assignments/Practical work.

The hardware and software platforms should be such that students can comfortably develop and run programs on those machines.

Since hardware and software evolve and change very rapidly the schools shall need to upgrade them as required. Following are the minimal specifications as of now.

RECOMMENDED FACILITIES:

- A lecture cum demonstration room with a MULTIMEDIA PROJECTOR/ an LCD and Overhead Projector (OHP) attached to the computer.
- A white board with white board markers should be available.

- A fully equipped Computer Laboratory that allows one computer per student.
- The computers should have a minimum of 1 GB RAM and at least a P - IV or Equivalent Processor.
- Good Quality printers.
- A scanner, a web cam/a digital camera (Should be provided if possible).

SOFTWARE

Any suitable Operating System can be used. For teaching fundamental concepts of computing using object-oriented approach, Blue J environment (3.2 or higher version) compatible with JDK (5.0 or higher version) as the base or any other editor or IDE, compatible with JDK (5.0 or higher version) as the base may be used. Ensure that the latest versions of software are used.

Mind Map : Function

Function

```
class Abc
{
    void sum (int a, int b )
{
    int c = a+b;
    system.out.println (c);
}
    psvm()
  {
    Abc of = new Abc (); object creation
    ob.sum(5, 6) function calling
  }
}
```

- Function Definition → void sum (int a, int b)
- Non Return Data type → void
- Function Definition → int c = a+b; system.out.println (c);
- Actual Parameter → 5, 6

String:
Sequence of characters.

- String s = "this is a cat" (indexes 0 1 2 3 4 5 6 7 8 9 10 11 12)
- Indexex of string starts with O.
  System.out.println(s.charAt(3));
  Output: s

Function overloading:
It is a process having more than one function of the same name.
Static Variables are class variable and Non static variables are Data members.

Constructor→special type of function having same Name as of the class. No return type not even void.

Array:

- set of similar types of data.
- Indexes start with O.
- Single dimentional.
- 2D Array
- int a[] = New int [5]; Array declaration Statement
- int a[] = {2, 3, 5, 7}; Array initialization statement
- int m[][]= new int [2] [3]; 112D Array

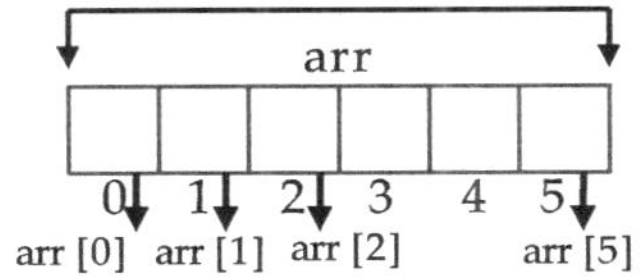

arr: 0 1 2 3 4 5 — arr [0] arr [1] arr [2] arr [5]

Mind Map : Introduction to Java

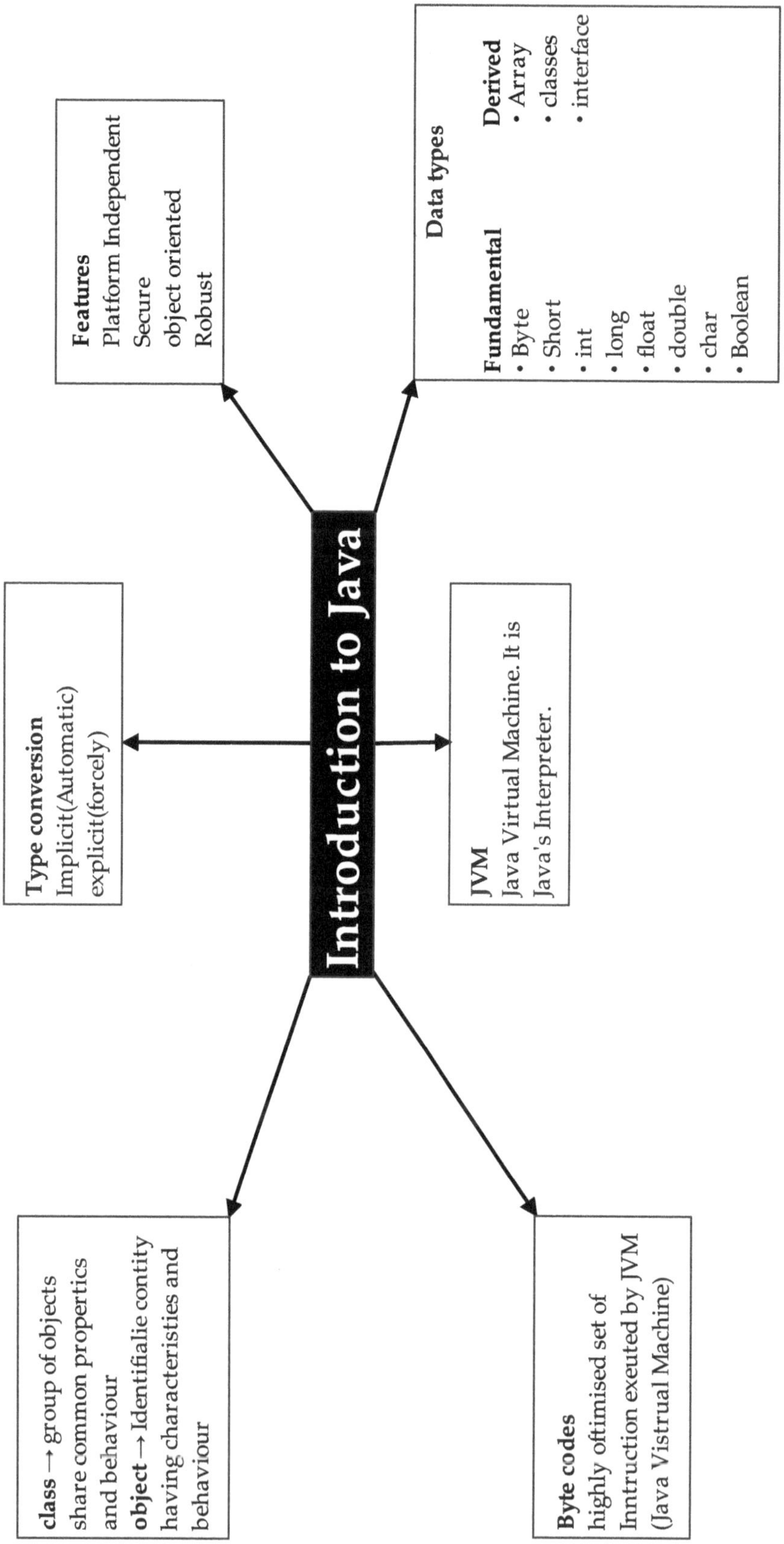

Introduction to Java

class → group of objects share common propertics and behaviour
object → Identifialie contity having characteristies and behaviour

Type conversion
Implicit(Automatic)
explicit(forcely)

Features
Platform Independent
Secure
object oriented
Robust

Byte codes
highly oftimised set of Inntruction exeuted by JVM (Java Vistrual Machine)

JVM
Java Virtual Machine. It is Java's Interpreter.

Data types

Fundamental
- Byte
- Short
- int
- long
- float
- double
- char
- Boolean

Derived
- Array
- classes
- interface

Mind Map :Decision Making Statement

Decision Making Statement

Difference between if and switch
if
if can value every type of value.
if can check multuple condition.

Switch
it can check only char and int type It can single condition.

Switch case
```
switch(choice)
{
case 1:
Statements;
break;
case 2:
statements;
break ;
default:
System.out,Println("Invoid choice");}
```

If else
```
If (num%2==0)
System.out.printer('Even')
else
system.out.printer("out");
```

Fall through:
when break statement missing in switch case

Dangeling else= when else cant find its scope between two if statement
```
    if(condition )
    if (condition )
              statement 1;
else
              statement 2;
```
c=(a:b)? a:b equivalent to the following statement
```
if          (a>b)
            c=a;
            c=b
```

Noted if: if with in if
```
If (condition)
{       if (condition)
            statement;
}
```

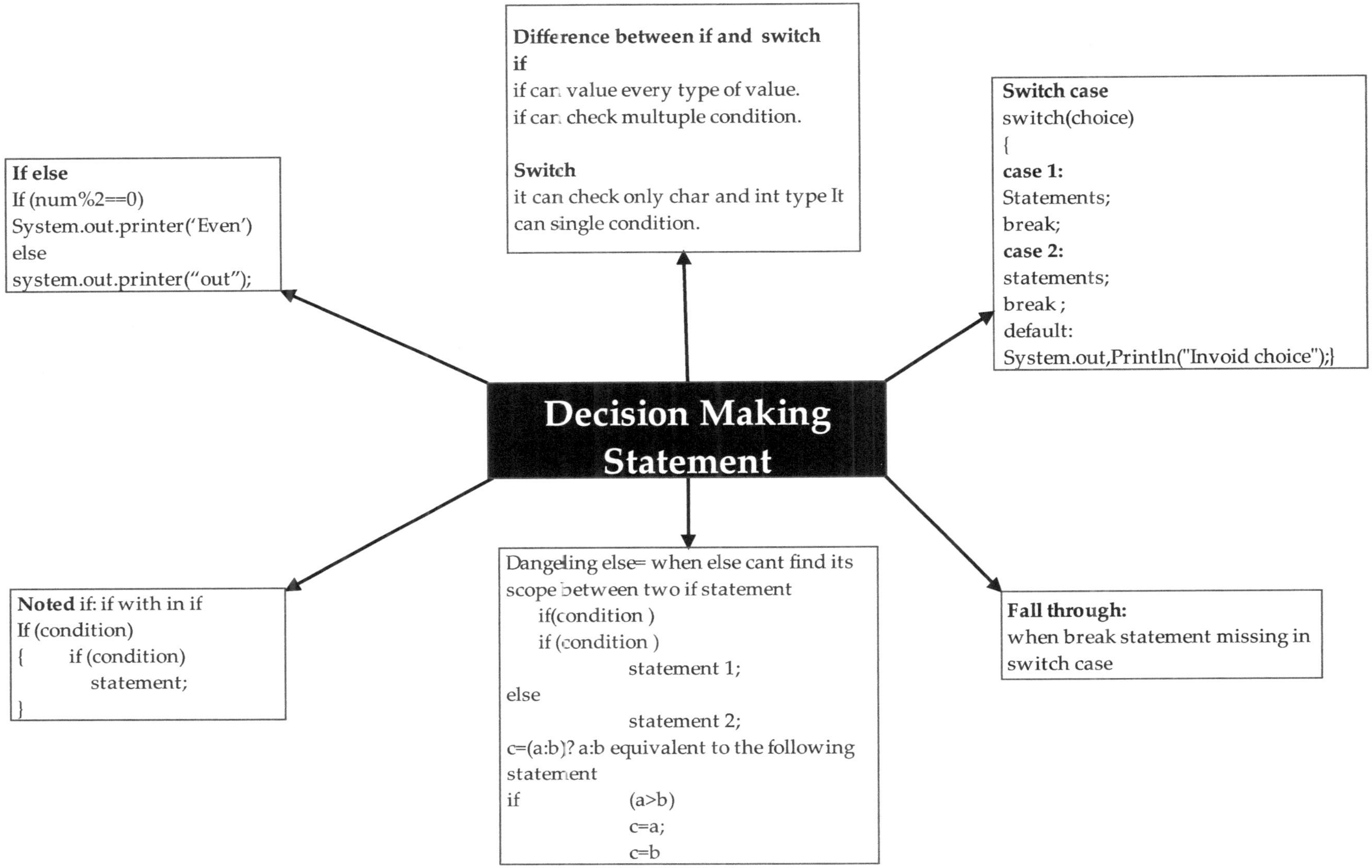

Mind Map : Iteration / Looping

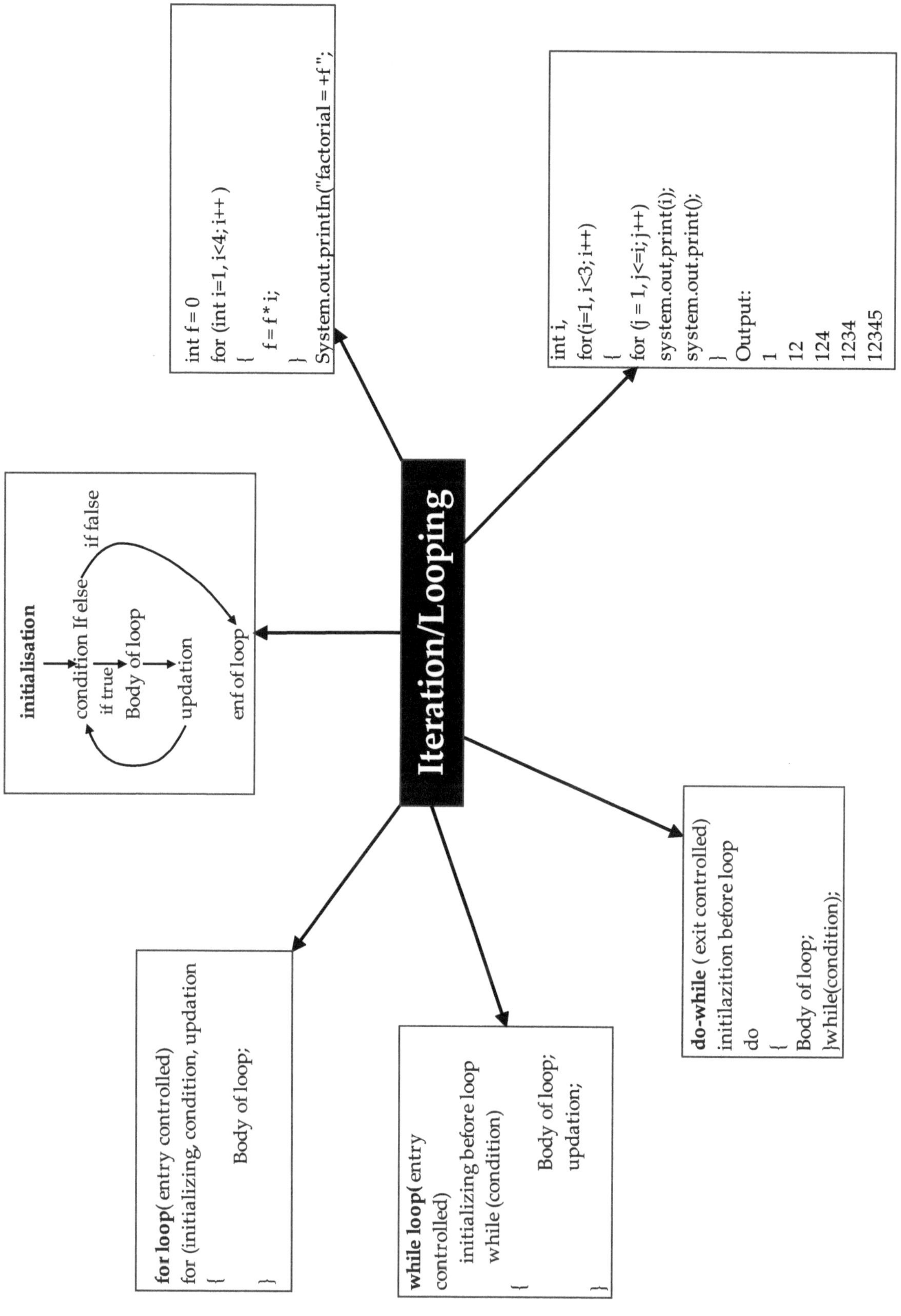

Iteration/Looping

initialisation
↓
condition If else → if false → enf of loop
if true ↓
Body of loop
↓
updation → (back to condition)

enf of loop

```
int f = 0
for (int i=1, i<4; i++ )
{
  f = f * i;
}
System.out.printIn("factorial = +f ";
```

```
int i,
for(i=1, i<3; i++)
{
for (j = 1, j<=i; j++)
system.out,print(i);
system.out.print();
}
```

Output:
1
12
124
1234
12345

for loop(entry controlled)
for (initializing, condition, updation
{
Body of loop;
}

while loop(entry controlled)
initializing before loop
while (condition)
{
Body of loop;
updation;
}

do-while (exit controlled)
initilazition before loop
do
{
Body of loop;
}while(condition);

SOLVED SAMPLE PAPER

ICSE 2023 EXAMINATION
SPECIMEN QUESTION PAPER
COMPUTER APPLICATIONS

Maximum Marks: 100
Time allowed: Two hours

Answers to this Paper must be written on the paper provided separately.
You will not be allowed to write during the first 15 minutes.
This time is to be spent in reading the question paper.
The time given at the head of this Paper is the time allowed for-writing the answers: -

This Paper is divided into two Sections.
Attempt all questions from Section *A* and any four questions from Section *B*.
The intended marks for questions or parts of questions are given in brackets [].

SECTION - A (40 Marks)
(Attempt all question from this section)

Question 1.

Choose the correct answer and write the correct. **[20]**

(i) Wrapping up data and methods together as one unit is termed as:

(a) Inheritance

(b) Polymorphism

(c) Encapsulation

(d) Abstraction

Answer: (c)

(ii) The datatype which is specified that the method does not return a value is:

(a) Void

(b) void

(c) VOID

(d) Boolean

Answer: (b)

(iii) The logical operator ______ is a unary operator:

(a) &&

(b) ||

(c) !

(d) >>

Answer: (c)

(iv) The Scanner class is a________ class.

(a) Primitive

(b) Derived

(c) Wrapper

(d) super class

Answer: (b)

(v) Math.pow(625,1/2) + Math.sqrt(144)

(a) 17.0

(b) 13.0

(c) 37.0

(d) 13

Answer: (b) as 1/2 = 0 in java.

(vi) The correct if statement for the following ternary operation statement is:

System.out.println(n%2= =0 ? "true":"false");

(a) if (*n*%2 == 0)

return true;

else

return false;

(b) if(n%2 = 0)

return "true";

else

return "false";

(c) if(n%2 = 0)

System.out.println("true");

else

System,out.println("false");

(d) if (n%2 = 0)

return false;

else

return false;

Answer: (c)

(vii) Multiple branching statement of java is:

(a) For

(b) while

(c) do... while
(d) switch
Answer: (d)

(viii) The number of bytes occupied by the constant 45 is:
(a) Four bytes
(b) Two bytes
(c) Eight bytes
(d) One byte
Answer: (a)

(ix) do.....while loop is an
(a) Entry controlled loop
(b) Infinite loop
(c) Exit controlled loop
(d) Finite loop
Answer: (c)

(x)
```
for (k = 1; k <= 2; k + +)
{
   for (m = 1; m <= 4; m + +)
   {
   System.out.println(m*2);
   }
}
```
How many times the inner loop is executed?
(a) 4 times
(b) 8 times
(c) 2 times
(d) 16 times
Answer: (b)

(xi) A method with the same name as the class and with arguments and no return data type is termed as:
(a) Parameterized constructor
(b) Default constructor
(c) Non-parameterized constructor

(d) Wrapper class method

Answer: (a)

(xii) int res=' A'; What is the value of res?

(a) A

(b) 66

(c) 65

(d) 97

Answer: (c) ASCII of 'A'

(xiii) The style of expressing single line comment is:

(a) /* comment*/

(b) * comment

(c) // comment

(d) /* comment

Answer: (c)

(xiv) The method to check if a character is an alphabet or not is:

(a) isLetter(char)

(b) isAlpha(char)

(c) isUppercase(char)

(d) isLowercase(char)

Answer: (a)

(xv) The output of DoubleparseDouble("71.25") +0.75 is:

(a) 72

(b) 72.0

(c) 71.0

(d) 71.75

Answer: (b)

(xvi) The method to convert a string to upper case is:

(a) toUpperCase(char)

(b) toUPPERCASE(String)

(c) toUpperCase(String)

(d) touppercase(String)

Answer: (c) but no is correct as toUpperCase does not take any argument.

(xvii) The output of the method "DETERMINATION".substring (2, 6) is:

(a) "TERM"

(b) term

(c) "Term"

(d) "TERMI"

Answer: (a)

(xviii) The array int $x[10]$ occupies:

(a) 10 bytes

(b) 40 bytes

(c) 20 bytes

(d) 80 bytes

Answer: (b) as one integer occupies 4 bytes

(xix) The element in $x[4]$ of the array $\{3, 5, 7, 12, 16, 18, 20, 35, 42, 89\}$ is:

(a) 16

(b) 12

(c) 7

(d) 18

Answer: (a)

(xx) Name the type of error that occurs for the following statement:

System.out.println(Math.sqrt(24 – 25));

(a) Syntax error

(b) Run time error

(c) Logical error

(d) No error

Answer: (d) as it will not terminate unexpectedly. But output will be NaN (not a number)

Question 2.

(i) Evaluate the expression: **[2]**

z+= a++ + --b+ ++a+ --b;

where a = 10, b = 5, Z = 10

Solution:

z = z + (a++ + --b+ ++a+ --b);

z = 10 + (10 + 4 + 12 + 3)

z = 29

(ii) Write java expression for: $|x^2 + xy|$ **[2]**

Solution:

Math.abs(Math.pow$(x, 2)$ $+$ x $*$ y)

(iii) Rewrite the following using ternary operators: **[2]**

if $(x > y)$

c = 'A';

else

$c ='a'$;

Solution:

char c $=$ $(x > y)$? 'A': 'a';

(iv) Rewrite the following while loop using for loop: **[2]**

int $x = 5$;

while ($x <= 5$)

{

$x++$;

}

System.out.println (x);

Solution:

int x;

for($x = 5$; $x <= 5$; $x++$)

{

$x++$;

}

System.out.println (x);

(v) How many times the following loop will gets executed? What is the output of the same? **[2]**

int counter=1;

do

{

System.out.println(counter);

} while (counter ++< 5);

Solution:

Values of counter variable:

counter = 1, after body of loop first condition checked then increment i.e. true

counter = 2, after body of loop first condition checked then increment i.e. true counter = 3, after body of loop first condition checked then increment i.e. true

counter = 4, after body of loop first condition checked then increment i.e. true

counter = 5, after body of loop first condition checked then increment i.e. false

Loop will be executed 5 times

Output:

1
2
3
4
5

(vi) "MISSISSIPPI".replace('S', 't').toLowerCase() **[2]**

Solution:

Mittittippi

(vii) "REDUCE".compareTo("REVOLT") + "ANTARTICA".lastIndexOf('A') **[2]**

Solution:

-10

As first dissimilar charaters in "REDUCE" and "REVOLT" are D and V and difference of their ASCII = -18. Then value of lastIndex of 'A' in "ANTARTIKA" is 8 and $-18 + 8 = -10$.

(viii) Define autoboxing with an example. **[2]**

Solution:

It is the process of automatically converting a fundamental (primitive) type to its corresponding wrapper class object.

Example: Integer obj = new Integer("533");

(ix) Consider the following program and answer the questions given below: **[2]**

```
class sample
{ int a, b;
sample(int x, int y)
{
        a = x; b = y;
}
void calculate()
{
  int z;
```

```
    z = a + b;
    System.out.println(z);
  }
  }
```

(a) Name the global variables.

Answer: 'a' and 'b'

(b) What are the method variables?

Answer: **'z'** as it is declared in method calculate and accessable with in it only.

(x) Consider the following array and answer the questions given below: **[2]**

int $x[\ ] = \{23, 45, 67, 12, 45, 89, 24, 12, 9, 7\}$

(a) What is the size of the array?

(b) What is the position of 89?

Solution:

(a) size of the array = 10 (number of elements in the array)

(b) 5th position or index

SECTION - B (60 marks)

(Attempt any four questions)

Question 3.

Define a class with the following specifications: **[15]**

Class name: Employee

Member variables: eno - employee number

ename - name of the employee

age - age of the employee

basic - basic salary

[Declare the variables using appropriate data types]

Member methods:

void accept() - accept the details using scanner class

void calculate () - to calculate the net salary as per the given specifications:

net = basic + hra + da $- pf'$

hra = 18.5% of basic

da = 17.45% of basic

pf = 8.10% of basic

if the age of the employee is above 50 he/she gets an additional allowance of Rs. 5000.

void print() - to print the details as per the following format

eno ename age, basic net

void main() - to create an object of the class and invoke the methods

Solution

```
import java.util.*;
class Employee
{
    long eno;
    String ename;
    int age;
    double basic;
    void accept()
  {
     Scanner sc = new Scanner(System.in);
     System.out.println("Enter Employee Number");
     eno = sc.nextLong();
     System.out.println("Enter Employee Name");
     ename = sc.nextLine();
     System.out.println("Enter Employee age");
     age = sc.nextInt();
     System.out.println("Enter Basic salary");
     basic = sc.nextDouble();
  }
  void calculate()
  {
     double hra = (18.5/100)*basic;
     double da = (17.45/100)*basic;
     double pf = (8.10/100)*basic;
     double net = basic + hra + da - pf;
     if(age > 50)
        net = net + 5000;
     System.out.println(net);
  }
  void print()
  {
      System.out.println("Employee Number\tEmployee Name\tAge\tBasic Salary\tNet
  Salary");
     System.out.print(eno+"\t"+ename+"\t"+age+"\t"+basic+"\t");
     calculate();
  }
```

```
    public static void main()
    {
        Employee ob = new Employee();
        ob.accept();
        ob.print();
    }
}
```

Question 4.

Define a class to overload the method print as follows: **[15]**

void print ()– to print the format

```
1
2  3
4  5  6
7  8  9  10
```

boolean print (int n) – to check whether the number is a Dudeney number, a number is dudeney if the cube of the sum of the digits is equal to the number itself.
Eg : $512 = (5 + 1 + 2)3 = (8)3 = 512$

void print (int a, char ch) - if $ch = s$ or S print the square of the number else if ch = c or C print the cube of the number.

Solution:

```
class Overload
{
    void print()
    {
        int i,j,a = 1;
        for(i=1;i<=4;i++)
        {
            for(j=1;j<=i;j++)
            {
                System.out.print(a+"\t");
                a++;
            }
            System.out.println();
        }
    }
    void print(int n)
    {
```

```
    int rem,sum=0,copy=n;
    while(n!=0)
    {
       rem=n%10;
       sum=sum+rem;
       n=n/10;
    }
    if(Math.pow(sum,3)==copy)
       System.out.println("Dudeney number");
    else
       System.out.println("Not Dudeney number");
  }
  void print(int a,char ch)
  {
    if(ch=='s' || ch=='S')
       System.out.println(Math.pow(a,2));
    else if(ch=='c' || ch=='C')
       System.out.println(Math.pow(a,3));
  }
}
```

Question 5.

Define a class to accept 10 integers and arrange them in descending order using bubble sort. Print the original array and the sorted array. **[15]**

Solution:

```
import java.util.*;
class Bubble
{
  public static void main()
  {
  Scanner sc = new Scanner(System.in);
  int arr[] = new int[10];
  int i,j,temp;
  System.out.println("Enter no's in array");
  for(i = 0; i < 10; i + +)
  {
    System.out.println("Enter ");
```

```
      arr[i]=sc.nextInt();
    }
    System.out.println("Array before Sorting:");
    for(i = 0; i < 10; i + +)
    {
      System.out.print(arr[i]+", ");
    }
    for(i = 0; i < 10; i + +)
    {
      for(j = 0; j < 9 – i; j + +)
        {
          if(arr[j]<arr[j+1])
          {
            temp=arr[j];
            arr[j]=arr[j+1];
            arr[j+1]=temp;
          }
        }
      }
    System.out.println("Array after Sorting:");
    for(i = 0; i < 10; i + +)
    {
      System.out.print(arr[i]+", ");
    }
    }
}
```

Question 6.

Define a class to accept values into a double array of size 20 and print the range of the array, range is the difference between the largest and the smallest elements of the array. **[15]**

Solution:

```
import java.util.*;
class Difference
{
  public static void main()
  {
    Scanner sc = new Scanner(System.in);
```

```
        double arr [] = new double[20];
        int i;
        System.out.println("Enter elements");
        for(i = 0; i < 20; i + +)
        {
          System.out.println("Enter ");
          arr[i] = sc.nextDouble();
        }
        double lar =  arr[0];
        double sml=arr[0];
        for(i = 0; i < 20; i + +)
        {
          if(arr[i]>lar)
            lar=arr[i];
          if(arr[i]<sml)
            sml=arr[i];
        }
        double diff=lar-sml;
        System.out.println("Difference of the array is"+diff);
      }
    }
```

Question 7.

Define a class to accept a string and print the same in reverse, also print the number of vowels in the string, **[15]**

Eg: S = "BEAUTIFUL"

Output - "LUFITUAEB"

No. of vowels = 5

Solution:

```
import java.util.*;
class StringReverse
{
  public static void main()
  {
    Scanner sc=new Scanner(System.in);
    String str, v="AEIOU",revstr="";
    int i,l,count=0;
```

```
        System.out.println("Enter String");
        str=sc.nextLine().toUpperCase();
        l =str.length();
        for(i=0;i<l;i++)
        {
            char ch=str.charAt(i);
            revstr=ch+revstr;
            if(v.indexOf(ch)!=-1)       //ch is a vowel
                count++;
        }
        System.out.println(revstr);
        System.out.println("Number of vowels = "+count);
    }
}
```

Question 8.

Define a class to accept the names of 10 students in an array and check for the existence of the given name in the array using linear search, if found print the position of the name, if not found print the appropriate message. Also, print the names which begins with the word "SRI". **[15]**

Solution:

```
import java.util.*;
class Linear
{
    public static void main()
    {
        Scanner sc=new Scanner(System.in);
        String name[]=new String[10],search;
        int i,flag = 0,count = 0;
        System.out.println("Enter elements");
        for(i=0;i<10;i++)
        {
            System.out.println("Enter ");
            name[i]=sc.nextLine().toUpperCase();
        }
        System.out.println("Enter a name to search");
        search=sc.nextLine().toUpperCase();
        for(i=0;i<10;i++)
```

```
      {
         if(name[i].startsWith("SRI"))
            count++;
         if(search.equals(name[i]))
         {
            flag=1;
         }
      }
      if(flag==1)
         System.out.println("Name found at "+(i+1)+"th position");
      else
         System.out.println("Name not found in the list");
      System.out.println("Names starts with \"SRI\""+count);
   }
}
```

ICSE 2023 EXAMINATION
SAMPLE PAPER- 1
COMPUTER APPLICATIONS

Maximum Marks: 100

Time allowed: Two hours

Answers to this Paper must be written on the paper provided separately.

You will not be allowed to write during the first 15 minutes.

This time is to be spent in reading the question paper.

The time given at the head of this Paper is the time allowed for-writing the answers: -

This Paper is divided into two Sections.

Attempt all questions from Section A and any four questions from Section B.

The intended marks for questions or parts of questions are given in brackets [].

SECTION - A (20 Marks)
(Attempt all question from this section)

Question 1.

Choose the correct answers to the questions from the given s. (Do not write the question, write the correct answer only.) **[20]**

(i) Which is default java package:

(a) java.lang

(b) java.util

(c) java.awt

(d) java.io

Answer: (a)

(ii) Which one is not a keyword in java?

(a) break

(b) default

(c) int

(d) true

Answer: (d)

(iii) What will be the output of the following code?

```
int ar [] = {2, 5, 8, 9, 1, 6, 4, 9, 3, 5 };
system.out.println(ar [3+4]};
```

(a) 6

(b) 7

(c) 9

(d) 5

Answer: (c)

(iv) Act of combining of data and its associated functions into a single unit is known as __________

(a) Polymorphism
(b) Encapsulation
(c) Inheritance
(d) Data abstraction
Answer: (b)

(v) Which visibility modifier gives the least access?
(a) Public
(b) Private
(c) Protected
(d) None
Answer: (b)

(vi) What will be output of the following statement?
String a = "Computer";
String b = "Applications";
System.out.println(a.compareTo(b));
(a) true
(b) false
(c) 2
(d) – 2
Answer: (c)

(vii) System.out.println("ProGRam".charAt(4));
(a) r
(b) G
(c) R
(d) A
Answer: (c)

(viii) A variable that is bounded to the object itself is called:
(a) Instance
(b) class
(c) Argument
(d) local
Answer: (a)

(ix) Write the correct output of the following code:
String str = "This is a cat";
System.out.println(str.indexOf(str.charAt(11));
(a) a

(b) 11
(c) 8
(d) T
Answer: (c)

(x) If, arr[ ] = {2, 4, 7, 9, 3; what is arr[2]
(a) 4
(b) 2
(c) 9
(d) 7
Answer: (d)

(xi) Which keyword is used to converts a variable into constant, whose value can't be change at any stage in the program?
(a) const
(b) final
(c) static
(d) None of these
Answer: (b)

(xii) "A" is a ____________ literal.
(a) String
(b) boolean
(c) integer
(d) character
Answer: (a)

(xiii) Which function is used to find the square root of negative number?
(a) abs()
(b) cbrt()
(c) sqrt()
(d) none
Answer: (d)

(xiv) What is the output given by the following code

```
Scanner sc = new Scanner(System.in);
int a[ ] = {2,5,3,7};
String str="Programmming is fun";
System.out.println(Math.abs(str.indexOf('z'))+a[a.length-1]);
```

(a) 6
(b) 8
(c) 5
(d) 4

Answer: (b)

(xv) What is the final value stored in variable x?
double a = – 8.35;
double x = Math.abs(Math.floor(a));
(a) 9.0
(b) 7.0
(c) 6
(d) 7
Answer: (a)

(xvi) Which is the default java package?
(a) java.awt
(b) java.io
(c) java.lang
(d) java.util
Answer: (c)

(xvii) What is the index of element 'i' in the following array:
char $ch[\,]$ = {'a', 'e', 'i', 'o', 'u}
(a) 3
(b) 2
(c) 1
(d) None
Answer: (b)

(xviii) Give the output of the following code:
System.out.println("Better".startsWith("Bet"));
(a) true
(b) false
(c) Bet
(d) None
Answer: (a)

(xix) The block which traps and handles the exception is known as_________
(a) default
(b) try
(c) final
(d) catch
Answer: (d)

(xx) System.out.println("A" + 2.5 * 2);
(a) A2.52

(b) A5.0
(c) A2.5*2
(d) None
Answer: (b)

Question 2.

(i) Name any two wrapper classes. **[2]**
Solution:
Integer for int and Double for double.

(ii) What is the difference between a break statement and a continue statement when they occur in a loop? **[2]**
Solution:
When break statement occur in a program it takes out control form the current loop.
When continue statement occur in a program it skips the remaining part of the loop and continue from the next iteration.

(iii) Write statements to show how finding the length of a character array chr [] differs from finding the length of a String object str. **[2]**
Solution:
To find the length of array chr []:
int len = chr.length;
To find the length of String str:
int len = str.length( );

(iv) Name the Java keyword that: **[2]**
(a) Indicates that a method has no return type.
(b) Stores the address of the currently - calling object.
Solution:
(a) void
(b) this

(v) What is an exception? **[2]**
Solution:
Exceptions are unexpected situations which may occur during execution of the program.
EXAMPLE: int c = 10/0;
The above statement has DivideByZero exception

Question 3.

(i) Write a Java statement to create an object mp4 of class Digital. **[2]**
Solution: Digital Mp4= new Digital ().

(ii) Identify the statements listed below as assignment, increment, method invocation or object creation statements. **[2]**

(a) System.out.println("Java").

(b) Costprice = 457.50;

(c) Car hybrid = new Car ();

(d) Petrolprice++;

solution:

(a) Method Invocation

(b) Assignment

(c) Object creation

(d) Increment

(iii) State the output of the following program segment: **[2]**

```
String str1 = "great"; String str2 = "minds";
System.out.println(strl.substring(0,2). concat(str2.substring(1)));
System.out.println(("WH" + (strl.substring(2).toUpperCase( ) ) )) ;
```

Solution:

Grinds

WHEAT

(iv) Give output of the following method: **[2]**

```
public static void main (String[ ] args)
{
        int a = 5;
        a++;
        System.out.println(a);
         a−= (a − −) − (− − a);
        System.out.println(a);
}
```

Solution:

$a = a - ((a --) - (-- a))$

$a = 6 - (6 - 4)$

$a = 4$

Output:

6

4

(v) Give the output of the following for the given array- **[2]**

int z [ ] = {39, 42, 36, 45, 75, 98 };

system.out.print(z[3] + "," + z[4] * 2);

Solution:

45 150

SECTION - B (60 Marks)
(Attempt any four questions from this section)

Question 4. **[15]**

Standard form of a **quadratic equation** is $ax^2 + bx + c = 0$. It has at most two solutions (roots) which may be real, equal, distinct or imaginary depending on the value of discriminant (D) = $b^2 - 4ac$. Print Nature of the roots of a quadratic equation whose coefficients (a, b and c) are given.

Design a class **Quadratic** with the following description:

Data Members:

double a, b, c : Coefficients of quadratic equation

double D : To store discriminant of a quadratic equation

Member Method:

(i) Quadratic () : Default constructor to initializes data members with their default values.

(ii) void input () : Take input in a, b and c

(iii) void print Nature () : Print nature of roots according to the following criteria:

If $b^2 - 4ac = 0$ then Roots are Real and Equal

If $b^2 - 4ac > 0$ then Roots are Real and Distinct

If $b^2 - 4ac < 0$ then Roots are Imaginary.

Write main( ) method also to create the object and call appropriate method to print the nature of a quadratic equation.

Solution:

```
import java.util.*;
class Quadratic
{
double a,b,c, D; //data Members
Quadratic()
{
        a=0.0;b=0.0;c=0.0;D=0.0;
}
void input() //Input in data memers
{
        Scanner sc=new Scanner(System.in);
        System.out.println("enter values of a, b and c");
        a=sc.nextDouble();
        b=sc.nextDouble();
        c=sc.nextDouble();
}
void printRoot()
{
```

```
            D=Math.pow(b,2)-4*a*c;
            if(D == 0)
                  System.out.println("Roots are Real and Equal");
            else if(D > 0)
                  System.out.println("Roots are real and Distinct");
            else
                  System.out.println("Roots are Imaginary");
      }
      public static void main()
      {
            Quadratic ob = new Quadratic();                    //Creating object
            ob.input();                                  //function calling
            ob.printRoot();
      }
}
```

Question 5. **[15]**

Write a program to input 'n' elements in an array and print the largest and the smallest number of the array. Also print their Difference.

Solution:

```
import java.util.*;
class LargeSmall
{
  public static void main( )
   {
     Scanner sc = new Scanner(System.in);
     int arr[ ],n,i;                           //declaration of array and variables
     System.out.println("Enter the limit for an array");
     n = sc.nextInt();
     arr=new int[n];
     System.out.println("Enter elements in an array");
     for(i=0 ; i<n ; i++)                       //input in array
     {
       System.out.println("Enter elements");
       arr[i]=sc.nextInt();
     }
     int sml=arr[0];
     int lar=arr[0];
     for(i = 0 ; i < n ; i ++)                        //finding largest and smallest elements
     {
       if(arr[i]>lar)
         lar=arr[i];
       if(arr[i]<sml)
```

```
        sml=arr[i];
    }
    System.out.println("Largest element is "+lar);
    System.out.println("Smallest element is "+sml);
    System.out.println("Difference = "+(lar - sml));
  }
}
```

Question 6. **[15]**

Write a program in java to accept a string in lower case and print all consecutive double characters

Sample input : I am f<u>ee</u>ding an a<u>pp</u>le to a ra<u>bb</u>it

Sample output : 3

Solution:

```
import java.util.*;
class Rabbit
{
public static void main( )
{
      Scanner sc = new Scanner(System.in);
      String str;
      int i, count = 0, len;
      System.out.println("Enter a string");
      str = sc.nextLine();
      len = str.length();                     //finding length of the string
      str = str.toLowerCase( );               //converting string into lower case
      for(i = 0 ; i < len - 1 ; i++)
      {
            char ch = str.charAt(i);
            char ch1 = str.charAt(i + 1);
            if(ch == ch1)                      //comparison of characters
                  count++;
      }
      System.out.println(count);
}
}
```

Variable description Table

S. No.	**Variable Name**	**Data types**	**Description**
1.	i	int	To operate for loop.
2.	count	int	For Counting purpose
3.	len	int	Storing length of a string

4.	str	String	Storing a string
5.	ch	char	Store extracted character from a string

Question 7. **[15]**

Write a code in java to initialize names of 5 countries with their capitals. Search for a name of the country input by the user using **BINARY SEARCH** technique. If the name of that country is found then print its corresponding capital otherwise print appropriate message.

Countries – AUSTRALIA, CANADA, CHINA, EGYPT, FRANCE, INDIA, JAPAN

Capitals – CANBERRA, OTTAWA, BEIJING, CAIRO, PARIS, NEW DELHI, TOKYO

Solution:

```
import java.util.*;
class Country
{
public static void main( )
{
        Scanner sc = new Scanner(System.in);
        String cn[ ] = {"AUSTRALIA","CANADA","CHINA","EGYPT","FRANCE",IN-
        DIA","JAPAN"};
        String cp[ ] = {"CANBERRA","OTTAWA","BEIJING","CAIRO", "PARIS","NEW
        DELHI", "TOKYO"};
        int i, l, low = 0, high= cn.length, flag = 0,mid = 0;
        System.out.println("Enter a Country name to search");
        String str = sc.nextLine();
        while(low <= high)
        {
                mid = (low + high)/2;                    //finding mid index of the string
        if(str.compareToIgnoreCase(cn[mid]) == 0)
        {
                flag = 1;
                break;
        }
        else if (str.compareToIgnoreCase(cn[mid]) > 0)
                        low = mid + 1;
        else
                        high = mid - 1;
}
if(flag == 1)
        System.out.println(cp[mid]);
else
        System.out.println("Country not found");
}
}
```

Question 8. **[15]**

Write a menu driven program to enter two numbers and perform the following task as per the user's choice

(a) Print HCF of both the numbers.

EXAMPLE: HCF OF 6 AND 15 = 3

(b) Print LCM of both the numbers.

EXAMPLE: LCM OF 6 AND 15 = 30

Solution:

```
import java.util.*;
class LcmHcf
{
public static void main()
{
  Scanner sc=new Scanner(System.in);
  int lcm=0,i,hcf=0,n1,n2,choice;
  System.out.println("enter two numbers");
  n1=sc.nextInt();
  n2=sc.nextInt();
  System.out.println("Enter 1 for LCM of two numbers");
  System.out.println("Enter 2 for HCF of two numbers");
  choice = sc.nextInt();
  switch(choice)
  {
    case 1:
      for(i=1;i<=n1*n2;i++)
      {
        if(i%n1==0 && i%n2==0)
        {
          lcm=i;
          break;
        }
      }
      System.out.println("LCM of "+n1+" and "+n2+" is "+lcm);
    break;
    case 2:
      for(i=1;i<=n1;i++)
      {
        if(n1%i==0 && n2%i==0)
        {
          hcf=i;
        }
      }
```

```
        System.out.println("HCF of "+n1+" and "+n2+" is "+hcf);
      break;
      default:
        System.out.println("Invalid choice");

          }
        }
      }
```

Question 9. **[15]**

Write a program to enter a sentence from the keyboard and count the number of times a particular word occurs in it. Display the frequency of the search word.

Solution:

```
import java.util.*;
class wordfreq
      {
      public static void main(String args[]) throws IOException
      {
            Scanner sc = new Scanner(System.in);
            String s,wrd,w = "';
            int len, count = 0;
            System.out.printin("enter a sentence");
            S = sc.nextLine().toUpperCase( );
            System.out.rintln("enter a word");
            wrd= sc.nextLine().toUpperCase( );
            len=s.length() :
            for(int i = 0; i <len;i++)
            {
                  char ch = s.charAt(i);
                  if(ch==(char)32)
                  {
                        if(w.equals(wrd))
                              count++;
                        w = "";
                        }
                  else
                        w = w + ch;
            }
            System.out.printin("Frequency of "+wrd+" = "+count);
        }
    }
```

ICSE 2023 EXAMINATION
SAMPLE PAPER- 2
COMPUTER APPLICATIONS

Maximum Marks: 100

Time allowed: Two hours

Answers to this Paper must be written on the paper provided separately.

You will not be allowed to write during the first 15 minutes.

This time is to be spent in reading the question paper.

The time given at the head of this Paper is the time allowed for-writing the answers: -

This Paper is divided into two Sections.

Attempt all questions from Section *A* and any four questions from Section *B*.

The intended marks for questions or parts of questions are given in brackets [].

SECTION - A (20 Marks)

(Attempt **all** question from this section)

Question 1.

Choose the correct answers to the questions from the given s. (Do not write the question, write the correct answer only.) **[20]**

(i) The access modifier that gives most access:

(a) package
(b) private
(c) protected
(d) public
Answer: (d)

(ii) According to java naming convention that is invalid:

(a) fnc( )
(b) fnc123( )
(c) 123fnc( )
(d) Fnc( )
Answer: (c)

(iii) which keyword is used to inform that an error has encountered?

(a) throws
(b) try
(c) break
(d) catch
Answer (a)

(iv) int res = 'a'

What is the value of res?

(a) 65
(b) 97

(c) a
(d) None
Answer: (b)

(v) What is the return type of the function compareTo( )
(a) boolean
(b) long
(c) String
(d) int
Answer: (d)

(vi) Which function is used to compare two strings lexicographically
(a) equals( )
(b) compareTo( )
(c) max( )
(d) equallexico( )
Answer: (b)

(vii) What will be the output of the following code?
int $x[\,] = \{4, 8, 2, 6\};$
int $y[\,] = \{6, 9, 4, 8\};$
system.out.print($x[2] + y[3]$);
(a) 10
(b) 5
(c) 12
(d) 28
Answer: (a)

(viii) classes are grouped together to make a:
(a) function
(b) array
(c) package
(d) None
Answer: (c)

(ix) How many bytes are consumed by the following array in memory?
int arr[ ] = new int[10];
(a) 10 bytes
(b) 20 bytes
(c) 40 bytes
(d) 80 bytes
Answer: (c)

(x) long $x = 30, y = 40;$
String A, B;
A = String.valueOf (x);
B = String.valueOf (y);
System.out.println($A + B$);
(a) 70
(b) 3040
(c) 1200
(d) 4030
Answer: (b)

(xi) What is the return type of substring( ) method?
(a) boolean
(b) String
(c) char
(d) int
Answer: (b)

(xii) State the data type of p.
$p = \text{"}A\text{"} + 2.5 * 2;$
(a) double
(b) String
(c) int
(d) None
Answer: (a)

(xiii) What will happen if you compile and executed the following code?

```
for(int i = 1 ; i <= 4 ; i++)
{
        continue;
}
System.out.println(i);
```

(a) 0
(b) 4
(c) 5
(d) Compilation error
Answer: (d)

(xiv) Which method of Scanner class is used to accept the next token as long type?
(a) nextlong()
(b) nextlnt()

(c) nextLong()
(d) none
Answer: (c)

(xv) Which of these is a composite data type?
(a) int
(b) boolean
(c) String
(d) double
Answer: (c)

(xvi) Which is a non return data type?
(a) boolean
(b) static
(c) void
(d) class
Answer: (c)

(xvii) Which keyword is used to load pre defined classes stored in java library in the program?
(a) new
(b) import
(c) class
(d) static
Answer: (b)

(xviii) What output will be printed by the following code snippet, when executed?
```
for(int i=0;i<=4;i++)
{
        System.out.print((char)('A' + i));
}
```
(a) 01234
(b) ABCDE
(c) A0A1A2A3A4
(d) Compilation error
Answer: (b)

(xix) What is the output given by the following code
```
Scanner sc = new Scanner(System.in);
int a[] = {2,5,3,7};
String str="Programmming is fun";
System.out.println(Math.abs(str.indexOf('z')+a[a.length-1]));
```
(a) 6
(b) 8

(c) 5
(d) 4
Answer: (a)

(xx) Which of the following is a primitive data type?
(a) short
(b) String
(c) Integer
(d) Float
Answer: (a)

Question 2.

(i) Give two differences between **switch** statement and **if-else** statement. **[2]**

Solution:

Switch	if – else
1. switch can only check integer or character expressions.	if – else can check any type of expression. i.e., double, String, float etc.

(ii) What is an infinite loop? Write an infinite loop statement. **[2]**

Solution:

A loop which does not terminate ever and continues infinitely, called infinite loop.

EXAMPLE:

```
for(i = 1 ;  ; i++){
        System.out.println(i);}
```

It is an infinite loop as there is no condition and no breaking statement inside loop.

(iii) What is a constructor? When is it invoked? **[2]**

Solution:

A constructor is a special type of function which has same name as of the class. It does not return any value not even void. It is used to initialize the initial stage of the object.

If the invoked when the object of the class is created.

(iv) What is dangling else? Explain. **[2]**

Solution:

It is a situation when else cannot find its scope between two if statement.

EXAMPLE:

```
if(a > b)
if(c > d)
        Statement1;
else
        statement2.
```

Using { brackets we can resolve this situation.

(v) Which of the following are valid comments? **[2]**

(a) /* comment */

(b) /* comment

(c) // comment

(d) */ comment */

Solution:

(a) and (c)

Question 3.

(i) What will be the ouput of the following code? **[3]**

```
int ar [ ] ={2, 5, 8, 9, 1, 6, 4, 9, 3, 5 };
system.out.println(ar [3]*2 );
system.out.println( ar[4]+3 );
system.out.println( ar[6+2]*3 );
```

Solution:

18

4

9

(ii) Study the method and answer the given questions. **[2]**

```
public void sample Method()
{
  for int i = 0; i < 3; i + +)
  {
    for( int j = 0; j < 2; j + +)
    {
        int number = ( int )( Math. random 0 * 10);
        System.out.println(number);
    }
  }
}
```

(a) How many times does the loop execute?

(b) What is the range of possible values stored in the variable number?

Solution:

(a) 6 times

(b) 0 to 9

(iii) What will be the output when the following code segments are executed?

(a) **[2]**

```
String s = "1001".
int x = Integer.valueOf(s);
double y = Double.valueOf(s);
System.out.println(" x = " + x);
```

System.out.println(" y = " + y);

(b) **[1]**

System.out.println("The King said \ "Begin at the beginning\" to me.");

Solution:

(a) $x = 1001$
$y = 1001.0$

(b) The King said "Begin at the beginning" to me

(iv) Rewrite the following program segment using the if-else statements instead of the ternary operator. **[2]**

grade = (mark >= 90) ? "A":(mark >= 80)? "B" : "C";

Solution:

```
String grade;
if(mark >=  90)
        grade = "A";
else if(mark >=  80)
        grade = "B";
else
        grade = "C";
```

SECTION - B (60 Marks)
(Attempt any four questions from this section)

Question 4. **[15]**

Define a class BusFare that has the following class specification:

Data members/instance variables:

String bNum	-	to store bus number
String bName	-	to store passenger's name
int km	-	to store kilometers travelled
double fare	-	to store total fare

Member functions :

BusFare()	-	constructor to initialize num to 0, name to "", km to 0 and fare to 0.0
void input()	-	to input bus number, passenger's name and kilometer.
void calcFare()	-	to calculate bus fare for a customer according to given condition:

kilometers travelled (km)	Rate/km
First 10 km	Rs 8
More than 10 and less or equal 20 km	Rs 12
More than 20 and less or equal 30 km	Rs 18
More than 30 and less or equal 40 km	Rs 25
More than 40 km	Rs 40

void show() - to display details in the following format

Bus Number	**Name**	**Kilometers travelled**	**Fare**
....	....	....	....

Write a main( ) method to create an object and call appropriate methods.

Solution:

```
import java.util.*;
class BusFare
{
String bNum,bName;
int km;
double fare;
BusFare( )
{
        bNum=0;
        bName="";
        km=0;
        fare=0.0;
}
void input( )
{
        Scanner sc = new Scanner(System.in);
        System.out.println("Enter Bus Number");
        bNum=sc.nextLine( );
        System.out.println("Enter Passenger Name");
        bName=sc.nextLine( );
        System.out.println("Enter Distance");
        km=sc.nextInt( );
}
void calcFare( )
{
        if(km <= 10)
                fare = km*8;
        else if(km>10 && km <= 20)
                fare = 10 * 8 + (km – 10) * 12;
        else if(km>20 && km <=30)
                fare = 10 * 8 + 10 * 12 + (km – 20) * 18;
        else if(km > 30 && km <= 40)
                fare = 10 * 8 + 10 * 12 + 10 * 18 + (km – 30) * 25;
        else if(km > 40)
                fare = 10 * 8 + 10 * 12 + 10 * 18 + 10 * 25 + (km – 40) * 25;
}
void show()
```

```
        {
            System.out.println("Bus Number \t Name \t Kilometers travelled \t Fare")
            System.out.println(bName + "\t" + bName + "\t" + km + "\t" + fare);
        }
        public static void main( )
        {
            BusFare ob = new BusFare( );
            ob.input( );
            ob.calFare( );
            ob.show( );
        }
}
```

Question 5. **[15]**

Write a program to input integer elements into an array of size 20 and perform the following operations:

(i) Display sum of all the elements of the array.

(ii) Find the average of the elements of the array.

Solution:

```
import java.util.*;
class Largest
{
public static void main(String args[])
{
    Scanner sc = new Scanner(System.in);
    int arr[ ] = new int[20], i, sum = 0;
    double avg;
    System.out.println("Enter numbers in the array");
    for(i = 0 ; i < 20 ; i++)                    //Input numbers in array
    {
        arr[i] = sc.nextInt( );
    }
    for(i = 0 ; i < 20 ; i++)
    {
        sum = sum + arr[i];
    }
    avg = (double)sum / 20;                      //typecasting int into double
```

```
            System.out.println("Sum of elements is " + sum);
            System.out.println("Average of elementsis " + avg);
    }
}
```

Question 6. **[15]**

Write a program to enter a string. Print all words from the string which start with vowels.

Sample Input : Amrita is very intelligent student

Sample Output : Amrita intelligent

Solution:

```
    import java.util.*;
    class Vowels
{
    public static void main(String args[ ])
    {
        Scanner sc = new Scanner(System.in);
        String v = "AEIOUaeiou", str, w = "";
        int i, len;
        System.out.println("Enter a sentence”");
        str = sc.nextLine( );
        str = str + " ";                        //adding a space to the last of string
        len = str.length( );                    //finding length of the string
        for(i = 0 ; i < len ; i ++)
        {
            char ch = str.charAt(i);
            if(ch == ' ')
            {
                if(v.indexOf(w.charAt(0)) >= 0)
                    System.out.print(w + "  ");
                w = "";                         //initializing variable empty
            }
            else
              w = w + ch;                       //forming a word
        }

    }
}
```

Question 7. **[15]**

Write a program to input and store integer elements in a double dimensional array of size 3 × 3 and print all the elements of the 2D array along with sum of all even elements of the array.

Solution:

```
        import java.util.*;
        class Matrix
{
  public static void main()
  {
    Scanner sc = new Scanner(System.in);
    int mat[][]=new int[3][3],i,j,sum=0;
    System.out.println("Enter elements");
    for(i=0 ; i < 3 ; i++)
    {
       for(j=0 ; j<3 ; j++)
       {
          System.out.println("Enter:");
          mat[i][j] = sc.nextInt();
       }
    }
    for(i=0 ; i < 3 ; i++)
    {
       for(j=0 ; j<3 ; j++)
       {
          System.out.print(mat[i][j]+"\t");
          if(mat[i][j]%2==0)
             sum = sum + mat[i][j];
       }
       System.out.println();
    }
    System.out.println("Sum = "+sum);
  }
}
```

Question 8. **[15]**

Write a menu driven program to enter a number (N) and perform the following task as per the user's choice

(a) Print sum of the following series up to the value of n given by user.

$1 + (1 + 2) + (1 + 2 + 3) + \ldots\ldots.. + (1 + 2 + 3 + \ldots. N)$

EXAMPLE: VALUE OF N = 4

$1 + (1 + 2) + (1 + 2 + 3) + (1 + 2 + 3 + 4)$ (No need to print series)

SUM OF THE SERIES = 20

(b) Print sum of digits of the number (N).

Solution:

```
import java.util.*;
class SumSeriesDigits
{
  public static void main()
  {
   Scanner sc=new Scanner(System.in);
   int i,j,sum=0,s=0,n=0,choice,rem;
   System.out.println("Enter a Number");
   n=sc.nextInt();
   System.out.println("Enter 1 for sum of the Series");
   System.out.println("Enter 2 for sum of digits");
   choice = sc.nextInt();
   switch(choice)
   {
     case 1:
       for(i=1;i<=n;i++)
   {
     s=0;
     for(j=1;j<=i;j++)
     {
       s=s+j;
     }
     sum=sum+s;
   }
   System.out.println("SUM IS "+sum);
   break;
  case 2:
   while(n!=0)
   {
```

```
            rem = n%10;
            sum = sum + rem;
            n = n/10;
        }
        System.out.println("SUM IS "+sum);
        break;
        default:
            System.out.println("Invalid choice");
    }
  }
}
```

Question 9. **[15]**

Write a program showing the concept function overloading using the following specifications:

void area(double r)	:	Find and Print area of circle (area= πr^2, Take = 3.14).
void area(double l, double b)	:	Find and Print area of rectangle (area = length * breadth).
void area(int s)	:	Find and print area of (area = side * side).

Write a main method to create an object and invoke the above methods.

Solution:

```
import java.util.*;
class Overload
{
    void area(double r)
    {
        double area;
        area = 3.14*r*r;
        System.out.println("Area of Circle "+area);
    }
    void area(double l, double b)
    {
        double area;
        area = l * b;
        System.out.println("Area of Rectangle "+area);
    }
    void area(int s)
    {
```

```
        int area;
        area = s*s;
        System.out.println("Area of Square "+area);
    }
    public static void main()
    {
        Scanner sc=new Scanner(System.in);
        System.out.println("Enter Radius of a circle");
        double rad=sc.nextDouble();
        System.out.println("Enter Length and breadth of a Rectangle");
        double l=sc.nextDouble();
        double b=sc.nextDouble();
        System.out.println("Enter side of a Square");
        int s=sc.nextInt();
        Overload ob=new Overload();
        ob.area(rad);
        ob.area(l,b);
        ob.area(s);
    }
}
```

UNSOLVED SAMPLE PAPER

ICSE 2023 EXAMINATION
SAMPLE PAPER- 1
COMPUTER APPLICATIONS

Maximum Marks: 100

Time allowed: Two hours

Answers to this Paper must be written on the paper provided separately.

You will not be allowed to write during the first 15 minutes.

This time is to be spent in reading the question paper.

The time given at the head of this Paper is the time allowed for-writing the answers: -

This Paper is divided into two Sections.

Attempt all questions from Section *A* and any four questions from Section *B*.

The intended marks for questions or parts of questions are given in brackets [].

SECTION - A (40 Marks)
(Attempt all question from this section)

Question 1.

Choose the correct answers to the questions from the given s. (Do not write the question, write the correct answer only.) **[20]**

(i) Which of these is not a primitive data type?

(a) int

(b) boolean

(c) String

(d) float

Answer: (c)

(ii) int b = 5/0; which type of error is this?

(a) Run time

(b) Compile time

(c) Syntax

(d) No error

Answer: (a)

(iii) Using encapsulation data and methods combines into ____________.

(a) package

(b) class

(c) object

(d) None of these

Answer: (b)

(iv) Which one is valid array declaration?

(a) int a[10]

(b) int a = new int [10]

(c) int a[ ] = new int[10]
(d) int a[10] = new int [10]
Answer: (c)

(v) Which of the following access specifiers makes the member visible to all?
(a) protected
(b) public
(c) private
(d) None
Answer: (b)

(vi) char *ch*[ ] = {'*a*','*e*','*i*','*o*','*u*'};
System.out.println((int)(ch[ch.length – 5]));
(a) 97
(b) *a*
(c) 0
(d) None
Answer: (a)

(vii) What is value of m from the following code segment:
String v = "aeiou", s = "Computer Application";
int m = v.indexOf(s.charAt(v.indexOf('o')));
(a) 1
(b) 3
(c) –1
(d) p
Answer: (c)

(viii) State the return of indexOf( ) function.
(a) boolean
(b) int
(c) char
(d) String
Solution: (b)

(ix) Which keyword distinguishes between instance variable and class variable?
(a) class
(b) static
(c) this
(d) final
Answer: (b)

(x) Choose the output of the following code segment:

char x = 'A'; int m;

m = (x == 'a') ? 'A' : 'a';

System.out.println("m = " + m);

(a) 97

(b) 65

(c) m = A

(d) m = 97

Answer: (d)

(xi) Which entity is called automatically when the object of the class is created?

(a) main( ) function

(b) Java virtual Machine

(c) constructor

(d) class itself

Answer: (c)

(xii) Which keyword is used to make a single copy of global variable, which shared between all the objects?

(a) public

(b) final

(c) static

(d) void

Answer: (c)

(xiii) Give output of the following Java code :

String str = "JAVA";

char ch = str.charAt(7/2);

int as = ch;

System.out.println((char)as);

(a) 65

(b) A

(c) a

(d) None

Answer: (b)

(xiv) Which of these is the correct format to create the character literal with value a.

(a) 'a'

(b) "a"

(c) new Character(a)

(d) \000a

Answer: (a)

(xv) Which function returns nearest even integer, in case its fractional part is .5, for example for 2.5 it returns 2.0 and for 7.5 it returns 8.0 etc.

(a) Math.round
(b) Math.rint
(c) Math.ceil
(d) None of the above
Answer: (b)

(xvi) The _____ operator is used to combine two or more expressions in such a way that it results true if all the expressions are true otherwise in false.

(a) &&
(b) ||
(c) >=
(d) !
Answer: (a)

(xvii) Which function is used to returns the largest integer less than or equal to a given number.

(a) Marh.rint
(b) Math.ceil
(c) Math.floor
(d) Math.round
Answer: (c)

(xviii) What is the output of the following code segment:

System.out.print("Hello!")
System.out.println("Java");

(a) Hello!Java
(b) Hello!Java
(c) Hello! Java
(d) None of the above
Answer: (a)

(xix) Choose the correct to arrange the operators as per their hierarchy.

* <= = ++

(a) * = ++ <=
(b) <= = * ++
(c) ++ * = <=
(d) ++ * <= =
Answer: (d)

(xx) Byte and boolean are _____ data types.

(a) Non primitive

(b) Primitive
(c) Reference
(d) None
Answer: (b)

Question 2.

(i) Define encapsulation. **[2]**

(ii) Explain the purpose of using a 'new' keyword in a Java program. **[2]**

(iii) What are literals? **[2]**

(iv) Mention the types of access specifiers. **[2]**

(v) What is constructor overloading? **[2]**

Question 3.

(i) Write the prototype of a function search which takes two arguments a string and a character and returns an integer value. **[2]**

(ii) Differentiate between = and == operators. **[2]**

(iii) What is the output of the following: **[2]**
String a="Java is programming language \n developed by \t\'James Gosling\'";
System.out.println(a);

(iv) Explain the use of the below given functions: **[2]**
(a) trim( )
(b) isWhitespace( )

(v) Given a character array: char chr[ ] = {'C', 'O', 'M', 'P', 'U', 'T', 'E', 'R' }; and an integer x = 3; **[2]**
What will be the output of the below statement if they are executed one after the other:
System.out.println(chr[x++]);
System.out.println(chr[x]++);

SECTION - B (60 Marks)
(Attempt any four questions from this section)

Question 4. **[15]**

Design a class name TelCall with the following member functions:

Date members:

int unit : Number of unit consumed by a person in a month.

double bill : Amount of bill paid by a person.

Member Functins:

TelCall() : Constructor, assign unit=0 and bill=0.0

void input() : Take input of units in unit variable.

void printBill() : Compute and print bill paid by a consumer according to the following slab.

Number of units	**Rate per unit**
1 to 50	` 5.0 per unit
51 to 100	` 6.5 per unit
above 100	` 8.0 per unit

Write a main() method to create the object object of TelClass and print bill by calling functions.

Question 5. **[15]**

Write a menu driven program to accept a number and check and display whether it is a prime number or not OR an automorphic number or not. (Use switch-case statement).

(a) Prime number : A number is said to be a prime number if it is divisible only by 1 and itself and not by any other number. Example : 3, 5, 7, 11, 13 etc.

(b) Automorphic number : An Automorphic number is the number which is contained in the last digit(s) of its square.
Example: 25 is an Automorphic number as its square is 625 and 25 is present as the last two digits.

Question 6. **[15]**

Write a program to accept s sentence and display those words only which starts with vowel

Question 7. **[15]**

Write a program to 25 telephone number in an array of numeric type and their owner names correspondingly in a string type array. Enter a name to search in the array. If the name present in the array, print the telephone number otherwise print an appropriate message. Use linear search technique.

Question 8. **[15]**

Write a program that encodes a word into Piglatin. To translate word into a piglatin word, convert the word into upper case and then place the first vowel of the original word as the start of the new word alongwith the remaining alphabets. The alphabets present before the vowel being shifted towards the end followed by "AY"

Sample Input1 : London

Sample Output1 : ONDONLAY

Sample Input2 : King

Sample Output2 : INGKAY

Question 9. **[15]**

Write a program to enter 10 elements in an array. Arrange them in ascending order by using **Bubble sort** technique.

ICSE 2023 EXAMINATION

SAMPLE PAPER- 2

COMPUTER APPLICATIONS

Maximum Marks: 100

Time allowed: Two hours

Answers to this Paper must be written on the paper provided separately.

You will not be allowed to write during the first 15 minutes.

This time is to be spent in reading the question paper.

The time given at the head of this Paper is the time allowed for-writing the answers: -

This Paper is divided into two Sections.

Attempt all questions from Section *A* and any four questions from Section *B*.

The intended marks for questions or parts of questions are given in brackets [].

SECTION - A (40 Marks)

(Attempt all question from this section)

Question 1.

Choose the correct answers to the questions from the given s. (Do not write the question, write the correct answer only.) **[20]**

(i) Which keyword is used to make a member of class sharable to all objects.

(a) public
(b) static
(c) import
(d) default

(ii) int a[ ] = {2, 4, 6, 8, 12};

System.out.println(a[a.length – 1]);
Output of this code:

(a) 2
(b) 12
(c) 4
(d) None of these

(iii) Which is not a keyword in java?

(a) public
(b) private
(c) protected
(d) friendly

(iv) The block which traps and handles the exception is known as __________

(a) default

(b) try

(c) catch

(d) finally( )

String s[ ] = {"India", "Japan", "America"};

(v) Statement to print the length of 'Japan':

(a) s[1].length;

(b) s(1).length( );

(c) s[1].length( );

(d) s[2].length( );

(vi) int arr[ ] = {2, 12, 6, 14, 9, 5};

int m = arr[4]%arr[arr.length – 1];

Value stored in m:

(a) 5

(b) 0

(c) 4

(d) 2

(vii) __________ is used to force an exception.

(a) throws

(b) throw

(c) final

(d) try

(viii) Give the output of the following statement:

System.out.println("Computer".endsWith("der"));

(a) false

(b) true

(c) 0

(d) –1

(ix) ________ members can be accessed only in the same class in which they are declared.

(a) private

(b) public

(c) protected

(d) data

(x) String str[ ] = {"Lucknow", "Kanput", "New Delhi", "Bombay"};

System.out.println(str[0].length( )>str[2].length( ));

(a) true
(b) false
(c) –1
(d) 0

(xi) How many bytes are reserved for double data type in Java?
(a) 4 bytes
(b) 6 bytes
(c) 8 bytes
(d) 16 bytes

(xii) If we don't use break in switch case, the situation is called
(a) polymorphism
(b) data abstraction
(c) fall through
(d) None of these

(xiii) Which one is a non-return data type?
(a) class
(b) int
(c) void
(d) Boolean

(xiv) What happens if there is no condition given in for loop?
(a) Compilation error
(b) Run time error
(c) Logical loop
(d) None of these

(xv) Name the type of error in the statement given below:
int $r = 100/0$;
(a) Syntax
(b) Runtime
(c) Logical
(d) None of the above

(xvi) Which type of value is returned by relational operators?
(a) int
(b) double
(c) char
(d) Boolean

(xvii) Which of these is not a primitive type in Java?

(a) array
(b) int
(c) boolean
(d) char

(xviii) Which statement is true?

1: If can be without else
2: else can be without if
(a) 1 is true
(b) 2 is true
(c) 1 and 2 both are true
(d) both are false

(xix) The first line of a function is known as ____________

(a) Function definition
(b) Function prototype
(c) Function signature
(d) None

(xx) Which one is odd in the following list?

break, continue, return, static
(a) break
(b) continue
(c) return
(d) static

Question 2.

(i) Define the term Byte code. **[2]**

(ii) What do you understand by type conversion?
How is implicit conversion different from explicit conversion? **[2]**

(iii) Name two jump statements and their use. **[2]**

(iv) What is Exception? Name two Exception Handling Blocks. **[2]**

(v) Write two advantages of using functions in a program. **[2]**

Question 3.

(i) What will be the output of the following code? **[2]**

int $m = 2$;

```
int n = 15;
for ( int i = 1; i < 5; i++);
                                        m++; --n;
System.out.println(" m = " + m);
System.out.println(" n = " + n);
char x = A';; int m;                                              [2]
m = (x =='a')? 'A': ' a'.
System.out.println(" m = " +m);
```

(ii) What will the following function return when executed? **[2]**

Math.max (−17, −19);

Math.ceil(7.8);

(iii) State the total size in bytes, of the arrays a [4] of char data type and p [4] of float data type. **[2]**

(iv) Name the keyword that: **[2]**

(a) Informs that an error has occurred in an input/output operation.

(b) Distinguishes between instance variables and class variables.

SECTION B (40 Marks)

(Attempt any four questions from this section)

Question 4. **[15]**

Define a class called **Mobike** with the following description:

Instance variables/data members:

Int bno	-	to store the bike's number
Int phno	-	to store the phone number of the customer
String name	-	to store the name of the customer
int days	-	to store the number of days the bike is taken on rent
int charge	-	to calculate and store the rental charge

Member methods:

void input( ) to input and store the detail of the customer.

void computer( ) - to compute the rental charge.

The rent for a bike Is charged on the following basis:-

First five days	-	Rs. 500 per day
Next five days	-	Rs. 400 per day
Rest of the days	-	Rs. 200 per day

void display( ) - to display the details in the following format:

Bike No.	Phone No.	Name	No. of days	Charge
---------	---------	---------	---------	---------

Write a main( ) method to create an object and call appropriate methods.

Question 5. **[15]**

Write a program to enter 10 mobile phone models (String type) and their price (double type) in two different arrays. Input a model if it present in the array, print its price along with model name (use linear search technique). Otherwise print an appropriate message (**Use Linear Search**).

Question 6. **[15]**

Write a menu driven program to perform the following: (Using switch case statement)
To print the series 0, 3, 7, 15, 24, ... n terms (Value of 'n' is an input by the user)
To find the sum of the series given below:
$S = 1/2 + 3/4 + 5/6 + 7/8 + \ldots .19/20$

Question 7. **[15]**

Write a program to input a number and print whether the number is a special number or not.
(A number is said to be a special number, if the sum of the factorial of the digits of the number is same as the original number)
Example : 145 is a special number, because 1! + 4! + 5! $= 1 + 24 + 120 = 145$
(Where ! stands for factorial of the number and the factorial value of a number is the product of all integers from 1 to that number, example 5! $= 1 * 2 * 3 * 4 * 5 = 120$)

Question 8. **[15]**

Write a program to enter age of 10 students in an array. Print their age in Tallest to shortest (**using Bubble sort technique**).

Question 9. **[15]**

Write a program to enter a string. Print the longest word along with its length.
For example: Honesty is the best policy
Longest word: Honesty
Length: 7

Answers:

Question 1:

(i) b	(ii) b	(iii) d	(iv) c	(v) c	(vi) c	(vii) b	(viii) a	(ix) a	(x) b
(xi) c	(xii) c	(xiii) c	(xiv) d	(xv) b	(xvi) d	(xvii) a	(xviii) a	(xix) b	(xx) d

ICSE 2023 EXAMINATION
SAMPLE PAPER - 3
COMPUTER APPLICATIONS

Maximum Marks: 100

Time allowed: Two hours

Answers to this Paper must be written on the paper provided separately.

You will not be allowed to write during the first 15 minutes.

This time is to be spent in reading the question paper.

The time given at the head of this Paper is the time allowed for-writing the answers: -

This Paper is divided into two Sections.

Attempt all questions from Section *A* and any four questions from Section *B*.

The intended marks for questions or parts of questions are given in brackets [].

SECTION - A (40 Marks)

(Attempt **all** question from this section)

Question 1.

Choose the correct answers to the questions from the given s. (Do not write the question, write the correct answer only.) **[20]**

(i) String str = "3";
System.out.println(Integer.parseInt(str)+ 'a');
(a) 3*a*
(b) 100
(c) 397
(d) None

(ii) What is return type of startWith( ) function?
(a) Int
(b) Boolean
(c) String
(d) None

(iii) Conversion of primitive type to its corresponding wrapper class object is called_____________
(a) Autoboxing
(b) Unboxing
(c) Type casting
(d) None

(iv) Block that always get executed, no matter which kind of exception is thrown.
(a) Finally
(b) Default
(c) Catch

(d) None

(v) Which package should be imported to use Scanner class

(a) Java.util
(b) Java.io
(c) Java.lang
(d) Java.awt

(vi) What is the output of the following code:

String s1 = "Amit", s2 = "Amita";

System.out.println(s1.compartTo(s2));

(a) – 97
(b) – 1
(c) 1
(d) 32

(vii) What should be the data type of 'y'?

y = (Math.sqrt(16) > 5.0) ? "true" : "false";

(a) Boolean
(b) String
(c) Int
(d) Double

(viii) Double $n = 15.245;$

String s = String.valueOf(n);
char ch = s.charAt(s.indexOf('.') + 1));
System.out.println(ch);

(a) 2
(b) 5
(c) 4
(d) 1

(ix) Which library function is used to returns nearest even integer in case of its fractional part is 0.5.

Example: $3.4 = 4.0, 6.5 = 6.0$ etc

(a) Round( )
(b) Random( )
(c) Ceil( )
(d) Rint( )

(x) Int arr[ ] = {1, 4, 8, 6, 12};
System.out.println("sum = " + arr[1] + arr[3]);
(a) Sum = 10
(b) Sum = 9
(c) Sum = 46
(d) 46

(xi) The ___________ are the words which have special meaning
(a) Keywords
(b) Identifier
(c) Methods
(d) Package

(xii) Which type of value is returned by logical operators?
(a) Int
(b) Boolean
(c) Char
(d) Double

(xiii) If an integer value can't store in int data type. Which data type is suitable for this value?
(a) Double
(b) Short
(c) Long
(d) Float

(xiv) if (a > b)
big = a;
else
big = b;
Which statement is correct replacement for this code?
(a) Big = (a > b) ? b : a;
(b) Big = (a > b) ? a : b;
(c) (a > b) ? big = a : big = b;
(d) None of these

(xv) Which keyword is used to create an instance of a class?
(a) This
(b) Import
(c) New
(d) Void

(xvi) Which loop executes at least once even the condition is false?
(a) For

(b) While
(c) Do while
(d) While and do – while both

(xvii) Method that accepts a string without any space is _______
(a) Next()
(b) Nextline()
(c) Nextint()
(d) None of the above

(xviii) Which one is correct arrangement in order of higher precedence to lower precedence?
(a) &&, %, >=, ++
(b) ++, %, >=, &&
(c) %, ++, >=, &&
(d) %, ++, &&, >=

(xix) How many primitive data types are used in java?
(a) 4
(b) 8
(c) 10
(d) 12

(xx) Which type of input is accepted by IF or ELSE IF statement?
(a) Int
(b) Boolean
(c) Char
(d) Float

Question 2.

(i) What is the difference between an object and a class? **[2]**

(ii) What does the token 'keyword' refer to in the context of Java? **[2]**

(iii) Give an example for keyword. **[2]**

(iv) State the difference between entry-controlled loop and exit controlled loop **[2]**

(v) What is difference between / and % operator? **[2]**

Question 3.

(i) Name the package that contains Scanner class.
Which unit of the class gets called when the object of the class is created? **[2]**

(ii) Give the output of the following: **[2]**

```
String n = "Computer Knowledge";
String m = "Computer Applications";
System.out.println(n.substring(0,8).concat(m.substring( 9)) );
System.out.println(n.endsWith("e"));
```

(iii) Write the output of the following: **[2]**

(a) System.out.println (Character.isUpperCase(' R '));

(b) System.out.println(Character.toUpperCase(' j'));

(iv) What is the role of keyword void in declaring functions? **[2]**

(v) Given that : int b[ ] = {2, 66, 76, 23, 78, 96}; **[2]**

SECTION - B (40 Marks)

(Attempt any four questions from this section)

Question 4. **[2]**

Define a class called **Library** with the following description:

Instance variables/data members

int accnum	-	Stores the accession number of the book
String title	-	Stores the title of the book
String author	-	Stores the name of the author

Member methods:

void input() : To input and store the accession number, title and author

void compute() : To accept the number of days late, calculate and display the fine charged as per the following table

No. of days (After seven days)	**Fine**
First three days	Rs. 2/day
Next 3 days	Rs. 4.0/day
After that	Rs. 5.0/day

void display() : To display the details in the following format:

Accession Number Title Author

Write a main method to create an object of the class and call the above member methods.

Question 5. **[15]**

Using the switch statement, write a menu driven program to:

(i) Generate and display the first 10 terms of Fibonacci series.

0, 1, 1, 2, 3, 5, . . .

The first two terms of Fibonacci series are 0 and 1 and each subsequent number is

the
sum of the previous two.

(ii) Find the sum of the digits of an integer that is input.
Sample Input: 32435
Sample Output: Sum of the digits = 18
For an incorrect choice, appropriate error message should be displayed.

Question 6. **[15]**

Write a program to perform **binary** search on a list of integers given below, to search for an element input
by the user, if it is found display the element along with its position, otherwise display the message
"Search element not found"
97, 89, 45, 30, 20, 15, 11, 9, 7, 5

Question 7. **[15]**

Write a program to enter two numbers. Check and print whether they are co – prime or not.
[Two numbers are said to be co – prime, if their HCF is 1]
EXAMPLE: Sample Input: 8, 9
Sample Output: They are co – prime.

Question 8. **[15]**

Write a program to enter 10 positive numbers in a single dimension array. Print factorial of all single digit numbers and sum of digits of remaining numbers.

Question 9. **[15]**

Write a program to enter a string and print it in reverse order.
Input : This is a cat
Output: Cat a is This

Answers:

Question 1:

(i) b (ii) b (iii) a (iv) a (v) a (vi) –1 (vii) b (viii) a (ix) d (x) c (xi) a (xii) (xiii) c (xiv) b(xv) c (xvi) c (xvii) a (xviii) b (xix) b (xx) b

ICSE 2023 EXAMINATION
SAMPLE PAPER - 4
COMPUTER APPLICATIONS

Maximum Marks: 100

Time allowed: Two hours

Answers to this Paper must be written on the paper provided separately.

You will not be allowed to write during the first 15 minutes.

This time is to be spent in reading the question paper.

The time given at the head of this Paper is the time allowed for-writing the answers: -

This Paper is divided into two Sections.

Attempt all questions from Section *A* and any four questions from Section *B*.

The intended marks for questions or parts of questions are given in brackets [].

SECTION - A (40 Marks)
(Attempt all question from this section)

Question 1.

Choose the correct answers to the questions from the given s. (Do not write the question, write the correct answer only.) **[20]**

(i) Which keyword is used to make a member of class sharable to all objects?

(a) Public

(b) Static

(c) Import

(d) Default

Answer: (b)

(ii) Given a character array char ch[ ] = {'J', 'A', 'V', 'A'} and an integer $a = 2$.

What will the output of the following statement?

System.out.println(ch[+ + a] + +);

(a) V

(b) A

(c) B

(d) 3

Answer(b)

(iii) What is the output of the following statement?

System.out.println(Character.toUpperCase('T'));

(a) T

(b) true

(c) 'T'

(d) Char

Answer: (a)

(iv) First index of an array is:

(a) 1
(b) 0
(c) – 1
(d) length(–1)
Answer: (b)

(v) What is the output of the following code segment?

System.out.println(57 – '0');

(a) 57
(b) 9
(c) 32
(d) None
Answer: (b)

(vi) Keyword which informs that an error has occurred in an input/output operation:

(a) Throw
(b) Throws
(c) Catch
(d) Try
Answer: (b)

(vii) Linear search can work on:

(a) Sorted array
(b) Unsorted array
(c) Both sorted and unsorted array
(d) None
Answer: (c)

(viii) What is the output of the following code segment:

double m = 12.5;
String s = String.valueOf(m);
System.out.println(s+2);

(a) 14.5
(b) 12.52
(c) 12.0
(d) None
Answer: (b)

(ix) String s[ ] = {"Lucknow" , "Kanpur", "Kolkata"};
System.out.println(s[0].charAt(s.length));

(a) K

(b) k
(c) P
(d) 3
Answer: (b)

(x) What is the output of the following code segment?
String s = "This is a book";
System.out.println(s.lastIndexOf((char)32));
(a) space
(b) 9
(c) 15
(d) 4
Answer: (b)

(xi) The ____________ allows a class to use the properties and methods of another class.
(a) Inheritance
(b) Polymorphism
(c) Encapsulation
(d) None of the above
Answer: (a)

(xii) Which loop(s) can be termed as entry controlled loop?
(a) For and while
(b) While and do – while
(c) For and do – while
(d) All of above
Answer: (a)

(xiii) Consider the following code:
```
Scanner sc = new Scanner(System.in);
System.out.println("Enter a string");
String str = sc.next( )
System.out.println(str.length( ));
```
If user type "It is a bird". Write the correct.
(a) 12
(b) 4
(c) 11
(d) No output
Answer: (a)

(xiv) Which one is ternary operator?
(a) ? *
(b) ? :

(c) : ?
(d) None of the above
Answer: (b)

(xv) Default value for boolean data type
(a) 1
(b) false
(c) 0
(d) True
Answer: (b)

(xvi) What happened when the following code is compile and run?

```
if(1)
{
System.out.println("HELLO");
}
```

(a) No output
(b) HELLO
(c) Compile time error
(d) None of these
Answer: (c)

(xvii) In the process of function overloading which changes need to be done to avoid error?
(a) Types of argument
(b) Number of argument
(c) Both (a) and (b)
(d) Either (a) or (b)
Answer: (d)

(xviii) Which loop is best if number of iterations are known.
(a) While
(b) Do – while
(c) For
(d) None of these
Answer: (c)

(xix) Choose the odd one:
(a) break
(b) continue
(c) return
(d) System.exit(0)
Answer: (b)

(xx) What is the result stored in 'x', after evaluating the following expression:

int $x = 5$; $x = x++ * 2 + 3 * --x$;

(a) 24
(b) 27
(c) 25
(d) 26
Answer: (c)

Question 2.

(i) What is meant by precedence of operators? **[2]**

(ii) What is a literal? **[2]**

(iii) State the Java concept that is implemented through: **[2]**
(a) A super class and a subclass
(b) The act of representing essential features without including background details.

(iv) Give a difference between a constructor and a method. **[2]**

(v) What are the types of casting shown by the following examples? **[2]**
(a) Double $x = 15.2$;
int y = (int)x;
(b) Int $x = 12$;
long $y = x$;

Question 3.

(i) Analyze the following program segment and determine how many times the loop will be executed and what will be the output of the program segment. **[2]**

```
int k = 1, i = 2;
while (+ + i < 6)
k *= i;
System.out.println(k);
```

(ii) Give the prototype of a function check which receives a character *ch* and an integer *n* and returns true or false. **[2]**

(iii) State the value of characteristic and mantissa when the following code is executed. **[2]**

```
String s = "4.3756".
int n =s. indexOf('.');
int characteristic = Integer.parseInt (s. substring (0, n));
int mantissa = Integer. valueOf (s.substring(n + 1) );
```

(iv) Write a statement each to perform the following task on a string: **[2]**

(a) Extract the second last character of a word stored in the variable *wd*.

(b) Check if the second character of a string *str* is in uppercase.

(v) Consider the following code: **[2]**

```
int sum(int num)
{?1? sum = 0;
while(num != 0)
{int rem = num % 10;
um = sum + ?2?;
um = num / 10;}
eturn sum; }
```

If the following code returns sum of digits of a number. Write the correct statement for ?1? and ?2?

Section - B (40 Marks)

(Attempt any four questions from this section)

Question 4. **[15]**

Design a class to overload a function compare ( ) as follows:

void compare(int, int) : to compare two integer values and print the greater of the two integers.

void compare (char, char) : to compare the numeric value of two character with higher numeric value.

void compare (String, String) : to compare the length of the two strings and print the longer of the two.

Question 5. **[15]**

Write a program to store the following names in an array. Enter a name to search in the array. If present

print its index otherwise print an appropriate message. Use **binary search** technique.

"Aman", "Amit", "Brijesh", "Danish", "Ekta", "John", "Mayank", "Ritesh", "Vishal", "Zishan"

Question 6. **[15]**

Write a program to enter a number. Check and print that it is a **Magic** number or not.

[Successive addition of digits of a number, until getting a single digit number. If the single digit is 1, the number is said to be **Magic Number**]

EXAMPLE:

SAMPLE INPUT: 298 is a Magic number as

$2+9+8 = 19$

$1 + 9 = 10$

$1 + 0 = 1$

When addition reaches in single digit, it is 1. So 298 is Magic.

Question 7. **[15]**

Design a class to overload a function printSeries( ) as follows:

(a) void printSeries(int n): to compute and print the sum of the following series.

$$1 + \frac{1+2}{1\times 2} + \frac{1+2+3}{1\times 2\times 3} + \cdots \ldots\ldots\ldots\ldots\ldots \frac{1+2+3+\cdots\ldots\ldots.+n}{1\times 2\times 3\times 4\ldots\ldots\ldots.\times n}$$

(b) void printSeries(String s): To print the string in the following format:

Example Input: Hello

Question 8. **[15]**

Write a program to enter names of 10 students. Convert them into upper case. Print their names

in lexicographic (a to z) order. (**Use bubble sort**)

EXAMPLE:

INPUT : Kiran, Naveen, Amit, Aman, Brijesh

OUTPUT : AMAN, AMIT, BRIJESH, KIRAN, NAVEEN

Question 9. **[15]**

Write a program to input a string in uppercase and print the frequency of each character.

Example: Input: HELLO WORLD

Output:

Characters	Frequency
D	1
E	1
II	1
L	3
O	2
R	1
W	1

ICSE 2023 EXAMINATION
SAMPLE PAPER - 5
COMPUTER APPLICATIONS

Maximum Marks: 100

Time allowed: Two hours

Answers to this Paper must be written on the paper provided separately.

You will not be allowed to write during the first 15 minutes.

This time is to be spent in reading the question paper.

The time given at the head of this Paper is the time allowed for-writing the answers: -

This Paper is divided into two Sections.

Attempt all questions from Section *A* and any four questions from Section *B*.

The intended marks for questions or parts of questions are given in brackets [].

SECTION - A (40 Marks)
(Attempt all question from this section)

Question 1.

Choose the correct answers to the questions from the given s. (Do not write the question, write the correct answer only.) **[20]**

(i) Give the output of the following code segment:

String n = "Computer Knowledge";
String m = "Computer Application";
System.out.println(n.substring(0, 8).concat(m.substring(9)));

(a) Computer Application
(b) ComputerApplication
(c) Computer knowledge
(d) None
Answer: (b)

(ii) t = Character.isUpperCase('5');

What should be the data type of t?

(a) int
(b) char
(c) boolean
(d) String
Answer: (c)

(iii) Int arr[ ] = {2, 4, 7,12, ,21, 9, 8, 13};

State the last index of the array.

(a) 8
(b) 7
(c) 13

(d)
(e) 9
Answer: (b)

(iv) String s = "Java is easy to learn"
System.out.println(s.indexOf(s.charAt(s.lastIndexOf(' '))));

(a) 4
(b) a
(c) J
(d) Y
Answer: (d)

(v) In java arrays are:
(a) Reference data type
(b) Primitive data type
(c) conditional type
(d) None
Answer: (a)

(vi) Output of the following code segment:
String s = "Examination";
System.out.println(s.startsWith(s.substring(5, s.length( ))));

(a) True
(b) False
(c) Nation
(d) Examin
Answer: (b)

(vii) Which feature can be implemented using encapsulation?
(a) Inheritance
(b) Data Abstraction
(c) Polymorphism
(d) Overloading
Answer: (b)

(viii) A variable declared in a class using static keyword is ___________ variable.
(a) Instance variable
(b) Class variable
(c) Local variable
(d) None
Answer: (b)

(ix) _______ is used to force an exception.

(a) throws

(b) throw

(c) final

(d) try

Answer: (a)

(x) What is the output of the following code segment?

```
int arr[ ] = {1, 2, 4, 6, 9, 3, 8}, sum = 0, i;

for(i=1 ; i< arr.length/2 ; i++)
sum = sum + arr[arr.length - i];
System.out.println(sum);
```

(a) 11

(b) 14

(c) 20

(d) 26

Answer: (a)

(xi) The process of automatic conversion of one type of data to another type is called __________.

(a) Autoboxing

(b) Explicit

(c) Implicit

(d) Data abstraction

Answer: (c)

(xii) What will happened when the following code will be compile and run?

```
int m = 5;
if(m <= 5)
System.out.print(Hello!");
System.out.print(" Java");
else
System.out.print("Error!");
```

(a) Error!

(b) Compile time error

(c) Hello! Java

(d) Hello!

Answer: (b)

(xiii) Which keyword is used to differentiate between data members and class variables?

(a) this
(b) static
(c) import
(d) new
Answer: (b)

(xiv) break statement is used to break from the current ______
(a) If statement
(b) Loop
(c) Switch case statement
(d) B and c both
Answer: (d)

(xv) When else cannot find its scope between two if statements, the situation is known as:
(a) Nested else
(b) Dangling else
Answer: (b)

(xvi) What is the output of following expression if x = 2 initially?

```
x+= x++ + ++x/2;
System.out.print(x);
```

(a) 6
(b) 7
(c) 5
(d) 8
Answer: (a)

(xvii) Which should be the data type of 'a' in the following statement?

```
a = "" + 2.4 * 2;
```

(a) int
(b) double
(c) String
(d) Float
Answer: (c)

(xviii) After compilation which code is generated by java compiler?
(a) Source code
(b) Object code
(c) UNICODE
(d) Byte code
Answer: (d)

(xix) How many times statement 1 will be executed?

```
for(int i = 2; i <= 9; i++)
{break;if(i % 2 == 0)
statement 1;}
```

(a) 5
(b) 4
(c) 1
(d) 0
Answer: (a)

(xx) When there are multiple definitions with the same function name present in a class, the concept is known as

(a) Data abstraction
(b) Inheritance
(c) Function overloading
(d) Encapsulation
Answer: (c)

Question 2.

(i) Define encapsulation. **[2]**

(ii) Explain the term object using an example. **[2]**

(iii) Define a variable. **[2]**

(iv) What is a wrapper class? Give an example. **[2]**

(v) What is the purpose of the new operator? **[2]**

Question 3.

(i) Analyze the following program segment and determine how many times the loop will be executed and what will be the output of the program segment. **[2]**

```
int p = 200;
while(true)
{if (p < 100)
break;
p = p – 20;}
 System.out.println(p);
```

(ii) What will be the output of the following code? **[2]**

(a) Int k = 5, j = 9;

```
k+= k + + − + + j + k;
System.out.println(" k = " + k);
System.out.println(" j = " + j);
```

(b) Double b = −15.6; **[2]**

```
Double a = Math.rint(Math abs(b));
System.out.println(" a = " + a);
```

(iii) Given that d[ ] [ ] = { { 4, 5, 6}, {1, 2, 3} }; **[2]**
What will be the value of d[0][2] and d[1][0] ?

(iv) Give the prototype of a function search which receives a sentence sentnc and a word wrd and returns 1 or 0 ? **[2]**

Section - B (40 Marks)
(Attempt any four questions from this section)

Question 4. **[15]**

Define a class **ElectricBill** with the following specifications:

Instance variable/data members:

String n : To store the name of the customer.
int units : To store the number of units consumed.
double bill : To srore the amount to be paid.

Member methods:

void accept() : To accept the name of the customer and number of units to be consumed
void calculate() : To calculate the bill as per the following tarrif:

Number of units	**Rate per units**
First 100 units	` 2.00
next 200	` 3.00
above 300 units	` 5.00

A surcharge of 2.5% charged if the number of units consumed is above 300 units.
void print(): To print the details as follows:
Name of the customer : ....
Number of units consumed : ....
Bill amount : ....
Write a main() method to create an object of the class and call the above member methods.

Question 5. **[15]**

Write a program to enter numbers in an array of 25 elements. Input a number and find and print the frequency of that number in the array **(Use Linear Search)**.

Question 6. **[15]**

Write a program to enter a number. Check and print that the number is Twisted prime or not.

[A number is said to be Twisted prime, if the new number obtained after reversing the digits is also a prime number.]

EXAMPLE: 13 is a twisted prime, as its reverse 31 is also a prime.

Question 7. **[15]**

Write a menu driven program to perform the following operation using switch-case:

(a) Input an integer number and print the greatest and the smallest digit present in the number.

Example:

Input: $n = 2943$

Output: Greatest digit = 9, Smallest digit = 2

(b) Input a line of text from the user and create a new word formed out of the first letter of the each word and convert the new word into uppercase.

Example:

Input: Present and past enquiry report.

Output: PAPER

Question 8. **[15]**

Write a program to enter a 2D array of 3 × 3 and print its Main diagonal only.

EXAMPLE:

```
              1  2  3                    1
INPUT:        4  5  6      OUTPUT:          5
              7  8  9                          9
```

Question 9. **[15]**

Write a program to enter a string and print * at place of vowels.

Example:

Input : Java is easy to learn

Output : J*v* *s **sy t* l**rn

PREVIOUS YEAR PAPER

ICSE 2019 EXAMINATION
PREVIOUS YEAR PAPER
COMPUTER APPLICATIONS

Maximum Marks: 100

Time allowed: Two hours

Answers to this Paper must be written on the paper provided separately.
You will not be allowed to write during the first 15 minutes.
This time is to be spent in reading the question paper.
The time given at the head of this Paper is the time allowed for-writing the answers: -

This Paper is divided into two Sections.
Attempt all questions from Section *A* and any four questions from Section *B*.
The intended marks for questions or parts of questions are given in brackets [].

SECTION - A (20 Marks)
(Attempt all question from this section)

Question 1.

(i) Name any two basic principles of object-oriented Programming. **[2]**

(ii) Write a difference between **unary** and **binary** operators. **[2]**

(iii) Name the keyword which: **[2]**
(a) Indicates that a method has no return type.
(b) Makes the variable as a class variable.

(iv) Write the memory capacity (storage size) of **short** and **float** data types in bytes. **[2]**

(v) Identify and name the following tokens: **[2]**
(a) Public
(b) 'a'
(c) ==
(d) {}

Solution.

(i) Abstraction and encapsulation are the basic principles of Object-oriented Programming.

(ii)

Unary Operators	Binary Operators
(i) The operators which act upon a single operand are called unary operators.	(i) The operators which require two operands for their action are called binary operators.

(ii) They are pre-increment and post increment (+ +)	(ii) They are mathematical operators and relational operators.

(iii)

(a) Void
(b) Static

(iv)

(a) Short: 2 bytes
(b) Float: 4 bytes

(v)

(a) Keyword
(b) Literal
(c) Operator
(d) Separator

Question 2.

(i) Differentiate between if else if and switch-case statements. **[2]**

(ii) Give the output of the following code: **[2]**

```
String P = "20", Q = "19",
int a = Integer .parselnt(P);
int b = Integer. valueOf(Q);
System.out.println(a+""+b);
```

(iii) What are the various types of errors in Java? **[2]**

(iv) State the data type and value of res after the following is executed: **[2]**

```
char ch = '9';
res = Character. isDigit(ch) ;
```

(v) What is the difference between the linear search and the binary search technique? **[2]**

Solution.

(i)

if else if	swith case
(i) It evaluates integer, character, pointer or floating-point type or boolean type.	(i) It evaluates only character or integer value.

(ii) Which statement will be executed depend upon the output of the expression inside if statement.	(ii) Which statement will be executed is decided by user.

(ii) 2019

(iii) Syntax error, Runtime error, Logical error

(iv) Boolean
True

(v)

Linear Search	Binary Search
(i) Linear search works both for sorted and unsorted data.	(i) Binary search works on sorted data (either in ascending order or in descending order).
(ii) Linear search begins at the start of an array i.e. at 0th position.	(ii) This technique divides the array in two halves, and the desired data item is searched in the halves.

Question 3.

(i) Write a Java expression for the following: **[2]**
$|x^2 + 2xy|$

(ii) Write the return data type of the following functions: **[2]**
(a) startsWith( )
(b) random( )

(iii) If the value of basic = 1500, what will be the value of tax after the following statement is executed? **[2]**
tax = basic > 1200? 200: 100;

(iv) Give the output of following code and mention how many times the loop will execute? **[2]**

```
inti;
for(i = 5; i >= l; i --)
{
    if(i%2 == 1)
    continue;
    System.out.print(i+ " ");
    }
```

(v) State a difference between call by value and call by reference. **[2]**

(vi) Give the output of the following: **[2]**

Math.sqrt(Math.max(9, 16))

(vii) Write the output for the following: **[2]**

String s1 = "phoenix"; String s2 ="island";
System.out.prindn (s1.substring(0).concat (s2.substring(2)));
System.out.println(s2.toUpperCase( ));

(viii) Evaluate the following expression if the value ofx=2,y=3 and z=1. **[2]**

v=x+–z+y+ + +y

(ix) String x[ ] = {"Artificial intelligence", "IOT", "Machine learning", "Big data"}; **[2]**

Give the output of the following statements:

(a) System.out.prindn(x[3]);
(b) System.out.prindn(x.length);

(x) What is meant by a package? Give an example. **[2]**

Solution.

(i) Math.abs((x * x) + (2 * x * y);

(ii) **(a)** boolean
(b) double

(iii) 200

(iv) 4 2
Loop will execute 5 times.

(v)

Call by value	Call by Reference
(i) In call by value the method creates its new set of variables (formal parameters) to copy the value of actual parameters and works with them.	(i) In call by reference, reference of the actual parameters is passed on to the method. No new set of variables is created.
(ii) Any change made in the formal parameter is not reflected in the actual parameter.	(ii) Any change made in the formal parameter is always reflected in the actual parameters.

(iii) Primitive data types are passed by call by value.	(iii) Reference types like (objects, array etc.) are passed by call by reference.

(vi) 4.0

(vii) phoenix land
ISLAND

(viii) = 2 + 0 + 3 + 4
$v = 9$

(ix)

(a) Big data
(b) 4

(x) A package is an organized collection of classes which is included in the program as per the requirement of the program. For example, java.io package is included for input and output operations in a program.

SECTION -B [60 Marks]
Attempt any four questions from this Section

Question 4. **[15]**

Design a class name ShowRoom with the following description:

Instance variables/ Data members:

String name – To store the name of the customer
long mobno – To store the mobile number of the customer
double cost – To store the cost of the items purchased
double dis – To store the discount amount
double amount – To store the amount to be paid after discount

Member methods: –

ShowRoom() – default constructor to initialize data members
void input() – To input customer name, mobile number, cost
void calculate() – To calculate discount on the cost of purchased items, based on following criteria

Cost	Discount (in percentage)
Less than or equal to ₹ 10000	5%
More than ₹ 10000 and less than or equal to ₹ 20000	10%
More than ₹ 20000 and less than or equal to ₹ 35000	15%

More than ₹ 35000	20%

void display () – To display customer name, mobile number, amount to be paid after discount

Write a main method to create an object of the class and call the above member methods.

Solution.

```
import java.util.*;
class ShowRoom
{
String name;
long mobno;
double cost;
double dis;
double amount;
ShowRoom( )
{
        name = " ";
        mobno =0;
        cost = 0.0;
        dis = 0.0;
        amount = 0.0;
        }
        void input( )
{
Scanner sc = new Scanner(System.in);
System.out.println("EnterName:");
name = sc.nextLine( );
System.out.println("Enter Mobile number:");
mobno = sc.nextLong( );
System.out.println("Enter cost:");
cost = sc.nextDouble( );
}
void calculate()
{
        if (cost <= 10000)
            dis cost*5.0/100.
        else if (cost > 10000 && cost < = 20000)
            dis = cost* 10.0/100.
        else if (cost > 20000 && cost < = 35000)
            dis = cost* 15.0/100;
        else if (cost > 35000)
            dis = cost*20.0/100.
        amount = cost – dis;
```

```
    }
    void display()
    {
        System.out.println("Name:" +name);
        System.out.println("Mobile No.:" +mobno);
        System.out.println("Amount::" +amount);
    }
    public static void main (String args( ))
    {
        ShowRoom obj = new ShowRoom( );
        obj.input( );
        obj.calculate( );
        obj.display( );
    }
    }
```

Question 5.

Using the switch-case statement, write a menu driven program to do the following: **[15]**

(a) To generate and print Letters from A to Z and their Unicode Letters Unicode

Letters	**Unicode**
A	65
B	66
.	.
.	.
.	.
Z	90

(b) Display the following pattern using iteration (looping) statement:

```
1
1 2
1 2 3
1 2 3 4
1 2 3 4 5
```

Solution.

```
import java.util.*;
class SwitchCase {
public static void main(String args[ ])
{
        Scanner sc = new Scanner (System.in);
        System.out.println("Enter 1 for Unicode:");
        System.out.prindn("Enter 2 for Pattern:");
        System.out.println("Enter your choice:");
        int choice = sc.nextlnt( );
        switch(choice)
```

```
{
        case 1:
                char ch;
                System.out.println( "Letters \t Unicode");
                for (ch = 'A'; ch< = 'Z'; ch+ +)
                {
                        System.out.println(ch +"\t" + (int)ch);
                }
                break.
        case 2:
                inti, j;
                for (i = 1; i< = 5; i+ +)
                {
                        for (j = 1; j < = i; j + +)
                        {
                                System.out.print(j + " ");.
                        }
                                System.out.println( );
                }
                break;
        default:
                System.out.println("Invalid Choice");
}
}
}
```

Question 6.

Write a program to input 15 integer elements in an array and sort them in ascending order using the bubble sort technique. **[15]**

Solution.

```
import java.util'*;
class BubbleAscend
{
public static void main(String args[])
 {
Scanner sc = new Scanner(System.in);
int i, j, temp;
int arr[ ] = new int[15];
System.out.println("Enter 15 integers:");
for (i = 0; i< = 15; i+ +)
{
        arr[i] = sc.nextlnt( );
}
```

```
    for(i = 0; i< 15; i++)
    {
        for(j = 0; j < 14 - i; j + +)
        {
            if(arr[j] >arr[j + 1])
            {
                    temp = arr[j];
                arr[j] = arr [j + 1];
                arr[j + 1] = temp;
            }
        }
}
System.out.println("Elements in ascending order are:");
for (i = 0; i< 15; i+ +)
{
        System.out.println(arr[i]);
}
}
}
}
```

Question 7.

Design a class to overload a function series () as follows: **[15]**

(a) void series (int x, int n) – To display the sum of the series given below:

$x^1 + x^2 + x^3 + \ldots\ldots\ldots\ldots\ldots\ x^n$ terms

(b) void series (int p) – To display the following series:

0, 7, 26, 63 p terms.

(c) void series () – To display the sum of the series given below:

$$\frac{1}{2}+\frac{1}{3}+\frac{1}{4}\ldots\ldots\ldots\ldots\ldots\frac{1}{10}$$

Solution.

```
import java.util.*;
class OverloadSeries
{
void series( int x, int n)
{
    int i; .
    double term=0.0;
    double sum = 0;
    for (i = 1; i< = n; i++)
    {
            term = Math.pow(x, i);
            sum = sum + term;
```

```
        }
        System.out.prindn("Sum:" +sum);
    }
    void series(int p)
    {
            int i;
            for (i = 1; i< = p; i++)
            {
                System.out.prindn((i * i * i) – 1 + " ");
            }
    }
    void series()
    {
        double i;
        double sum = 0;
            for (i =-2; i< = 10; i+ +)
            {
                sum= sum + 1/i;
            }
            System.out.println("Sum:" +sum);
}
}
```

Question 8.

Write a program to input a sentence and convert it into uppercase and count and display the total number of words starting with a letter 'A'. **[15]**

Example:

Sample Input: ADVANCEMENT AND APPLICATION OF INFORMATION TECHNOLOGY ARE EVER CHANGING.

Sample Output : Total number of words starting with letter A' = 4.

Solution.

```
import java.util.*;
class UpperCount
{
public static void main(String args[ ])
{
    int i,count=0;
    Scanner sc = new Scanner(System.in);
    String str;
    System.out.println("Enter sentence:");
    str = sc.nextLine().toUpperCase();
    str=" "+str;
    for(i=0 ; i<str.length() ; i++)
```

```
{
   char ch = str.charAt(i);
if(ch ==(char)32)
{
        if(str.charAt(i+1)=='A')
              count++;
}
}
System.out.println("Total number of words starting with letter 'A'::" +count);
}
}
```

Question 9.

A tech number has even number of digits. If the number is split in two equal halves, then the square of sum of these halves is equal to the number itself. Write a program to generate and print all four digit tech numbers. **[15]**

Example:

Consider the number 3025

Square of sum of the halves of 3025 $= (30 + 25)^2$

$= (55)^2$

$=$ 3025 is a tech number.

Solution.

```
import java.util.*;
class TechNumber
{
public static void main(String args[ ])
{
    int i, a, b, sum;
    String n;
    System.out.println("Four Digits Tech Numbers are");
    for(i=1000; i<=10000; i++)
    {
          n = i +"";
      a = Integer.parseInt(n.substring(0,2));
      b = Integer.parseInt(n.substring(2));
      sum = (int)Math.pow((a + b), 2);
      if (sum == i)
      System.out.println(i);
    }
}
}
```

ICSE 2020 EXAMINATION
PREVIOUS YEAR PAPER
COMPUTER APPLICATIONS

Maximum Marks: 100

Time allowed: Two hours

Answers to this Paper must be written on the paper provided separately.
You will not be allowed to write during the first 15 minutes.
This time is to be spent in reading the question paper.
The time given at the head of this Paper is the time allowed for-writing the answers: -

This Paper is divided into two Sections.
Attempt all questions from Section *A* and any four questions from Section *B*.
The intended marks for questions or parts of questions are given in brackets [].

SECTION – A (20 Marks)
(Attempt all question from this section)

Question 1.

(i) Define Java byte code. **[2]**

(ii) Write a difference between *class* and an *object*. **[2]**

(iii) Name the following: **[2]**
(a) The keyword converts variable into constant.
(b) The method terminates the entire program from any stage.

(iv) Which of the following are primitive data types? **[2]**
(a) double
(b) String
(c) char
(d) Integer

(v) What is an operator? Name any two types of operators used in Java. **[2]**

Solution:

(i) After java compilation source code converted into an intermediate code called Java byte code. It is then executed by the JVM (Java virtual machine). This code is platform independent.

(ii)

Class	Object
1. A class is a group of similar objects which share common properties and behavior. 2. Class is a blueprint or template from which abject is crated. 3. Class is crated using class keyword.	1. Object is a physical entity with some characteristics and behavior. 2. Object is an instance of a class 3. Object is crated using new keyword.

(iii)

(a) final

(b) System.exit(0);

(iv) double and char

(v) An operator is a special symbol that is used to perform various mathematical and logical expressions.

Example: +, *, >, && etc.

Question 2.

(i) What is autoboxing in Java? Give an example. **[2]**

(ii) State the difference between length and length() in Java. **[2]**

(iii) What is constructor overloading? **[2]**

(iv) What is the use of *import* statements in Java? **[2]**

(v) What is an infinite loop? Give an example. **[2]**

Solution:

(i) Autoboxing refers to the conversion of a primitive value into an object of the corresponding wrapper class.

Example: Integer obj = new Iteger(50);

(ii)

length	length()
1. Primarily used by java Array. 2. It is a property. 3. Returns number of elements in array.	1. Used by the String class 2. It is a function. 3. Returns number of characters including space in the String.

(iii) The constructor overloading can be termed as the concept of having more than one constructor with different parameters, so that every constructor can be used to create a different object.

(iv) An import statement is used to load certain predefined classes or the entire package in the program.

(v) A loop which never ends is called an infinite loop.
Example:
```
for (i = 1; i<=5 ; )
System.out.println(i);
```
Since updating statement is missing. So condition is once true always true.

Question 3.

(i) Write a Java expression for the following: **[2]**

$$\sqrt{b^2 - 4ac}$$

(ii) Evaluate the following if the value of $x = 7, y = 5$ **[2]**

$$x += x + + + x + + + y$$

(iii) Write the output for the following: **[2]**
```
String s1 = "Life is Beautiful";
System.out.println ("Earth" + s1.substring(4));
System.out.println( sl.endsWith("L"));
```

(iv) Write the output of the following statement: **[2]**
```
System.out.println("A picture is worth It A thousand words.);
```

(v) Give the output of the following program segment and mention how many times the loop will execute: **[2]**
```
int k;
for (k = 5; k <= 20; k+= 7)
if (k%6 == 0)
    continue;
System.out.println ( k );
```

(vi) What is the data type returned by the following library methods? **[2]**

(a) isWhitespace()

(b) compareTolgnoreCase()

(vii) Rewrite the following program segment using logical operators: **[2]**
```
if (x > 5)
if (x > y)
System.out.println (x + y);
```

(viii) Convert the following **if else if** construct into **switch case:** **[2]**
```
if ( ch ==' c' || ch = 'C' )
```

System.out · print("COMPUTER");
else if (ch= 'h' || ch = 'H')
System. out. print("HINDI");
else
System. out. print("PHYSICAL EDUCATION");

(ix) Give the output of the following: **[2]**
(a) Math.pow (36,0.5) + Math.cbrt (125)
(b) Math.ceil (4.2) + Math.floor (7.9)

(x) Rewrite the following using the **ternary** operator: **[2]**

$$\text{if } (n_1 > n_2)$$
$$r = \text{true};$$
$$\text{else } r = \text{false};$$

Solution:

(i) Math.sqrt(Math.pow(a,2)-4*a*c)

(ii) $x = 7, y = 5$
$x = x + (x++ + x ++ + y)$
$x = 7 + (7 + 8 + 6)$
$x = 28$

(iii) Earth is Beautiful
false

(iv) A picture is worth "A thousand words."

(v) 26, loop will execute 3 times.

(vi) **(a)** boolean
(b) int

(vii) if($x > 5$ && $x > y$)
System.out.println($x + y$);

(viii) switch(ch)
{
case 'c':
case 'C':

```
            System.out . print("COMPUTER");
        break;
        case 'h':
        case 'H':
            System.out . print('HINDI);
        break;
        default:
            System.out . print("PHYSICAL EDUCATION");
    }
```

(ix)

(a) 11.0

(b) 12.0

(x) $r = (n1 > n2)$? true : false;

SECTION - B(60 Marks)

Attempt any four questions from this Section

Question 4.

A private Cab service company provides service within the city at the following rates: **[15]**

	AC CAR	NON AC CAR
UPTO 5 KM	₹150/–	₹120/–
BEYOND 5 KM	₹10/–*PERKM*	₹08/– PER KM

Design a class **CabService** with the following description:

Member variables /data members:

Stringcar_type – Tostorethetypeofcar (ACorNONAC)

double km – Tostorethekilometertravelled doublebill – Tocalculateandstorethebillamount

Membermethods: – Defaultconstructortoinitializedatamembers.

CabService() Stringdatamembersto "n^{and} anddoubledata membersto 0.

0. voidaccept () – Toacceptcar_typeand km (usingScannerclass only).

void calculate 0 - To calculate the bill as per the rules given above.

void display0 - To display the bill as per the following format

CAR TYPE:

KILOMETER TRAVELLED:

TOTAL BILL:

Create an object of the class in the main method and invoke the member methods.

Solution:

```
import java.util.*;
class CabService
{
  String car_type;
  double km,bill;
  CabService()
  {
    car_type="";
    km=0.0;
    bill=0.0;
  }
  void accept()
  {
    Scanner sc = new Scanner(System.in);
    System.out.println("Enter Car Type");
    car_type = sc.nextLine().toUpperCase();
    System.out.println("Enter Kilometer ");
    km = sc.nextDouble();
  }
  void calculate()
  {
    if(km<=5 && car_type.equals("AC CAR"))
      bill = 150;
    else if(km<=5 && car_type.equals("NON AC CAR"))
      bill = 120;
    else if(km>5 && car_type.equals("AC CAR"))
    {
      bill = 150+(km-5)*10;

    }
    else if(km>5 && car_type.equals("NON AC CAR"))
    {
      bill = 120+(km-5)*8;
    }
  }
  void display()
  {
    System.out.println("CAR TYPE: "+car_type);
    System.out.println("KILOMETER TRAVELLED: "+km);
    System.out.println("TOTAL BILL : "+bill);

  }
  public static void main()
```

```
  {
    CabService ob = new CabService();
    ob.accept();
    ob.calculate();
    ob.display();
  }
}
```

Question 5.

Write a program to search for an integer value input by the user in the sorted list given below us ing **binary** search technique. If found display "Search Successful" and print the element, otherwise display "Search Unsuccessful" **[15]**

{31, 36, 45, 50, 60, 75, 86, 90}

Solution:

```
import java.util.*;
class BinarySearch
{
        public static void main( )
        {
                Scanner sc = new Scanner(System.in);
                int arr[ ] = {31, 36, 45, 50, 60, 75, 86, 90};
                int low=0, high = arr.length – 1, mid, flag = 0;
                System.out.println("Enter a number to search");
                ser = sc.nextInt( );
                while(low <= high)
                {
                        mid = (low + high)/2;                    //finding mid index of the string
                        if(arr[mid] == ser)
                        {
                                        flag = 1;
                                break;
                        }
                        else if (ser>arr[mid])
                                        low = mid + 1;
                        else
                                        high = mid - 1;
                }
                if(flag == 1)
                        System.out.println(ser + " found at " + mid + " index");
```

```
            else
                    System.out.println("Element not found");
        }
}
```

Question 6.

Write a program to input a **sentence** and convert it into uppercase and display each word in a separate line. **[15]**

Example	:	Input	:	India is my country
		Output	:	INDIA IS MY COUNTRY

Solution:

```
import java.util.*;
class SeparateLines
{
   public static void main()
   {
      Scanner sc = new Scanner(System.in);
      String str;
      int i,len;
      System.out.println("Enter a text");
      str = sc.nextLine().toUpperCase();
      len = str.length();
      for(i=0;i<len;i++)
      {
         char ch = str.charAt(i);
         if(ch == (char)32)
            System.out.println();
         else
            System.out.print(ch);

      }
   }
}
```

Question 7.

Design a class to overload a method Number( ) as follows: **[15]**

(i) void Number (int num, int d) - To count and display the frequency of a digit in a number.

Example:

$$num = 2565685$$
$$d = 5$$

Frequency of digit 5 = 3

(ii) void Number (int $n1$) - To find and display the sum of even digits of a number.

Example:

$$n1 = 29865$$

Sum of even digits = 16

Write a main method to create an object and invoke the above methods.

Solution:

```
import java.util.*;
class Overload
{
   void Number(int n, int d)
   {
      int count=0,rem;
      while(n!=0)
      {
         rem=n%10;
         if(rem==d)
            count++;
         n=n/10;
      }
      System.out.println("Frequency of digit "+d+" is "+count);
   }
   void Number(int n1)
   {
      int sum=0,rem;
      while(n1!=0)
      {
         rem=n1%10;
         if(rem%2==0)
            sum = sum + rem;
         n1=n1/10;
      }
      System.out.println("Sum of even digit   = "+sum);
   }
   public static void main()
   {
      Scanner sc = new Scanner(System.in);
      int num1,num2,digit;
      System.out.println("Enter a number and a digit");
      num1=sc.nextInt();
      digit = sc.nextInt();
      System.out.println("Enter a number for sum of even digits");
      num2=sc.nextInt();
      Overload ob = new Overload();
```

```
        ob.Number(num1,digit);
        ob.Number(num2);
    }
}
```

Question 8.

Write a menu-driven program to perform the following operations as per the user's choice: **[15]**

(i) To print the value of $c = a^2 + 2ab$, where **a** varies from 1.0 to 20.0 with an increment of 2.0 and $b = 3.0$ is a constant.

(ii) To display the following pattern using **for** loop:

A
AB
ABC
ABCD
ABCDE

Display proper message for an invalid choice.

Solution:

```
import java.util.*;
class Switch
{
  public static void main()
  {
    Scanner sc = new Scanner(System.in);
    int choice;
    System.out.println("Enter 1 to Print the values of an Expression");
    System.out.println("Enter 1 to Print the Pattern");
    choice = sc.nextInt();
    switch(choice)
    {
      case 1:
        double a, b=3.0, c=0;
        for(a=1.0 ; a<=20.0 ; a++)
        {
          c = Math.pow(a,2)+2*a*b;
          System.out.println("Value "+1+" = "+c);
        }
      break;
      case 2:
        char i,j;
        for(i='A' ; i<='E' ; i++)
        {
          for(j='A' ; j<=i ; j++)
            System.out.print(j);
```

```
                System.out.println();
            }
        default:
        System.out.println("Invalid choice");
      }
    }
  }
```

Question 9.

Write a program to input and store integer elements in a double-dimensional array of size 3 × 3 and find the sum of elements in the left diagonal. **[15]**

Example:

1 3 5
4 6 8
9 2 4

Output: Sum of the left diagonal elements = (1 + 6 + 4) = 11

Solution:

```
import java.util.*;
class Matrix
{
  public static void main()
  {
    Scanner sc = new Scanner(System.in);
    int mat[][]=new int[3][3],i,j,sum=0;
    System.out.println("Enter elements");
    for(i=0 ; i < 3 ; i++)
    {
      for(j=0 ; j<3 ; j++)
      {
        System.out.println("Enter:");
        mat[i][j] = sc.nextInt();
      }
    }
    for(i=0 ; i < 3 ; i++)
    {
      for(j=0 ; j<3 ; j++)
      {
        System.out.print(mat[i][j]+"\t");
        if(i == j)
          sum = sum + mat[i][j];
      }
    }
    System.out.println("Sum of left diagonal = "+sum);
```

```
    }
}
```

ICSE 2022 EXAMINATION
PREVIOUS YEAR PAPER
COMPUTER APPLICATIONS

Maximum Marks: 50

Time allowed: Two hours

Answers to this Paper must be written on the paper provided separately.

You will not be allowed to write during the first 15 minutes.

This time is to be spent in reading the question paper.

The time given at the head of this Paper is the time allowed for-writing the answers: -

This Paper is divided into two Sections.

Attempt all questions from Section *A* and any four questions from Section *B*.

The intended marks for questions or parts of questions are given in brackets [].

SECTION - A (20 Marks)
(Attempt all question from this section)

Question 1.

Choose the correct answers to the questions from the given s. (Do not write the question, write the correct answer only.)

(i) Return data type of isLetter(char) is

(a) Boolean

(b) boolean

(c) bool

(d) char

Answer: (b)

(ii) Method that converts a character to upper Case is

(a) toUpper( )

(b) toUpperCase( )

(c) toUppercase

(d) toUpperCase(char)

Answer: (d)

(iii) Give the output of the following String methods :

"SUCCESS".indexOf ('S') + "SUCCESS"lantIndexOf('S').

(a) 0

(b) 5

(c) 6

(d) – 5

Answer: (c)

(iv) Corresponding wrapper class of float data type is.

(a) FLOAT
(b) float
(c) Float
(d) Floating
Answer: (c)

(v) ________ class is used to convert a primitive date type to its corresponding Object.

(a) String
(b) Wrapper
(c) System
(d) Math
Answer: (b)

(vi) Give the output of the following code.

System. out. println("Good".Concat("Day"));

(a) GoodDay
(b) Good Day
(c) Goodday
(d) goodDay
Answer: (a)

(vii) A single dimensional array contains N elements. What will be the last subscript?

(a) N
(b) N - 1
(c) N - 2
(d) N + 1
Answer: (b)

(viii) The access Modifier that gives least accessibility is

(a) private
(b) public
(c) protected
(d) package
Answer: (a)

(ix) Give the output of the following code:

```
String A = "56.0", B = "94.0";
double C = Double.parseDouble(A);
double D = Double.parseDouble(B);
System.out.println((C +D));
```

(a) 100
(b) 150.0

(c) 100.0
(d) 150
Answer: (b)

(x) what will be the output of the following code ?
System.out.println("LuckNow".substring(0,4));
(a) Lucknow
(b) Luckn
(c) Luck
(d) luck
Answer: (c)

SECTION-B

(Attempt any four questions from this section)

Question 2.

Define a class to perform binary search on a list of integers given below to search for an element input by the users, if it is found display the element along with its position, Otherwise display the message "Search clement not found". **[10]**

2, 5, 7, 10, 15 , 20, 29, 30, 46, 50

Solution:

```
import java.util.*;
class BinarySearch
{
    public static void main( )
    {
        Scanner sc = new Scanner(System.in);
        int arr[ ] =  {2, 5, 7, 10, 15, 20, 29, 30, 46, 50};
        int low=0, high = arr.length – 1, mid, flag = 0;
        System.out.println("Enter a number to search");
        ser = sc.nextInt( );
        while(low <= high)
        {
            mid = (low + high)/2;                    //finding mid index of the string
            if(arr[mid] == ser)
            {
                    flag = 1;
                    break;
            }
            else if (ser>arr[mid])
                low = mid + 1;
            else
                high = mid - 1;
        }
```

```
        if(flag == 1)
            System.out.println(ser + " found at " + mid + " index");
        else
            System.out.println("Element not found");
        }
}
```

Question 3.

Define a classTo declare a character array of size ten, accept the character into the array and display the characters with highest and lowest ASCII (American standard code for information interchange) value. **[10]**

EXAMPLE:

'R', 'z', 'q', 'A', 'N', 'p', 'm', 'U', 'Q', 'F'

OUTPUT:

Character with highest ASCII value = z

Character with lowest ASCII value = A

Solution:

```
import java.util.*;
class BubbleSort
{
  public static void main()
  {
    Scanner sc = new Scanner(System.in);
    char chr[]=new char[10];
    int i,j;
    System.out.println("Enter Characters in the array");
    for(i=0 ; i<10 ; i++)
    {
      System.out.println("Enter :");
      chr[i]=sc.next().charAt(0);
    }
    for(i=0 ; i<10 ; i++)
    {
      for(j=0 ; j<9-i ; j++)
      {
        if(chr[j]>chr[j+1])
        {
          char temp = chr[j];
          chr[j]=chr[j+1];
          chr[j+1]=temp;
        }
      }
    }
```

```
        System.out.println("Character with highest ASCII value = "+chr[9]);
        System.out.println("Character with lowest ASCII value = "+chr[0]);
    }                   //end of main
}                       end of class
```

Question 4.

Define a class to declare an array of size 20 of double data type accept the elements into the array and perform the following **[10]**

(a) Calculate and print the product of all the elements

(b) Print the square of each element of the array

Solution:

```
import java.util.*;
class SumOfArray
{
    public static void main()
    {
        Scanner sc = new Scanner(System.in);
        int arr[]=new int[5];
        int i,j,prod=1;
        System.out.println("Enter Characters in the array");
        for(i=0 ; i<5 ; i++)
        {
            System.out.println("Enter :");
            arr[i]=sc.nextInt();
        }
        for(i=0 ; i<5 ; i++)
        {
            prod = prod * arr[i];
            System.out.println("Square of "+arr[i]+" = "+(int)Math.pow(arr[i],2));
        }
        System.out.println("Product of all elements = "+prod);
    }               //end of main
}                   //end of class
```

Question 5.

Define a class to accept a string and print the characters with uppercase and lowercase reversed but all the other characters should remain the same as before.

Example : INPUT: WelCoMe_2022

OUTPUT : wELcOmE_2022 **[10]**

Solution:

```
import java.util.*;
class ReverseCase
{
```

```
    public static void main()
    {
        Scanner sc=new Scanner(System.in);
        String str;
        int i,len;
        System.out.println("Enter a String ");
        str=sc.nextLine();
        len = str.length();
        for(i=0 ; i<len ; i++)
        {
            char ch = str.charAt(i);
            if(Character.isUpperCase(ch))
                ch = Character.toLowerCase(ch);
            else if(Character.isLowerCase(ch))
                ch = Character.toUpperCase(ch);
            System.out.print(ch);
        }
    }
}
```

Question 6.

Define a class to declare an array to accept and store 10 words. Display only those words which begin with the letter 'A' or 'a' and also and with the letter 'A' or 'a'. **[10]**

EXAMPLE:

Inputs: Hari, Anita, Akash, Amrita, Alina, Devi, Rishabh, John, Farha, AMITHA

Output:

Anita

Amrita

Alina

AMITHA

Solution:

```
class Array
{
    public static void main()
    {   Scanner sc=new Scanner(System.in);
        String name[]={"Hari", "Anita","Akash", "Amrita", "Alina", "Devi", "Rishabh", "John", "Farha",
        "AMITHA"};
        int i;
        for(i=0;i<name.length;i++)
        {
            String str=name[i];
            if(str.startsWith("A")||str.startsWith("a"))
                System.out.println(str);
```

```
        }
      }
    }
```

Question 7.

Define a class to accept two string of same length and form a new word in such a way that the first character of the first word is followed by the first character of the second word and so on.

EXAMPLE:

Input string 1- BALL

Input string 2- WORD

OUTPUT: BWAOLRLD **[10]**

Solution:

```
import java.util.*;
class Alternate
{
  public static void main()
  {
    Scanner sc = new Scanner(System.in);
    String s1,s2,w="";
    int i;
    System.out.println("Enter First String ");
    s1=sc.nextLine().toUpperCase();
    System.out.println("Enter Second String ");
    s2=sc.nextLine().toUpperCase();
    for(i=0;i<s1.length();i++)
    {
      char ch1=s1.charAt(i);
      char ch2=s2.charAt(i);
      w=w+ch1+ch2;
    }
    System.out.println(w);
  }
}
```

MOST EXPEXTED QUESTIONS PAPER

ICSE 2023 EXAMINATION
SAMPLE PAPER – 1
COMPUTER APPLICATIONS

Maximum Marks: 100

Time allowed: Two hours

Answers to this Paper must be written on the paper provided separately.

You will not be allowed to write during the first 15 minutes.

This time is to be spent in reading the question paper.

The time given at the head of this Paper is the time allowed for-writing the answers: -

This Paper is divided into two Sections.

Attempt all questions from Section *A* and any four questions from Section *B*.

The intended marks for questions or parts of questions are given in brackets [].

SECTION - A (40 Marks)
(Attempt all question from this section)

Question 1.

Choose the correct answers to the questions from the given s. (Do not write the question, write the correct answer only.) **[20]**

(i) Process of wrapping of data members and member functions into a single unit is called encapsulation. What is the single unit is called?

(a) Object

(b) Class

(c) Abstraction

(d) None

Answer: (b)

(ii) When you pass an array to a method, the method receives ___________

(a) A copy of the array

(b) A copy of the first element

(c) The reference of the array

(d) The length of the array

Answer: (c)

(iii) int arr[ ] = new int[0];

System.out.println(arr.length);

What is the result when the following code is compiling and running?

(a) Compilation error

(b) Run time error (program will terminate with some error message)

(c) 0

(d) None

Answer: (c)

(iv) Which one is invalid comment in java?

(a) // comment

(b) /*comment*/

(c) */comment*/

(d) None

Answer: (c)

(v) In java, a group of classes is called:

(a) Objects

(b) Encapsulation

(c) Package

(d) Array

Answer: (c)

(vi) Which will legally declare, construct and initialize an array?

(a) int a( ) = {1, 2, 3, 4};

(b) int a[ ] = (2, 3, 5, 6);

(c) int a[ ] = {2, 1, 6, 9, 8};

(d) int a[ ] = {1, 2.5, 8, 12};

Answer: (c)

(vii) Which of these method of string class can be used to test to strings for equality?

(a) isequal( )

(b) isequals( )

(c) equals( )

(d) equalsTo

Answer: (c)

(viii) String class is defined in which of these packages?

(a) java.lang

(b) java.util

(c) java.io

(d) java.string

Answer: (a)

(ix) In java how many bytes are consumed by the following array in memory ?

int arr[ ] = new int [15];

(a) 15

(b) 20

(c) 30

(d) 60

Answer: (d)

(x) What is the output of the following code segment?

```
String str = "Hello World";
System.out.println(str.indexOf('h'));
```

(a) 0
(b) 1
(c) – 1
(d) None
Answer: (c)

(xi) Name the statement/methods/keyword that causes the control to transfer back to a method call.

(a) System.exit(0)
(b) return
(c) continue
(d) break
Answer: (b)

(xii) What will be the value in variable 'f' after executing the following expression if a = 5 and $b = 3.$

int $a = 5, b = 3;$
int $f = (++a) * b++ - --a;$
System.out.print(f);

(a) 14
(b) 11
(c) 12
(d) 13
Answer: (d)

(xiii) When java source code is compiled, it is converted into a code called ________

(a) JVM
(b) output code
(c) byte code
(d) object code
Answer: (c)

(xiv) The entity with the same name as of the class and which does not have a return data type is called as

(a) Constructor
(b) Function
(c) Method
(d) Loop
Answer: (a)

(xv) Which keyword is used to skip the current iteration and continues to the next iteration, when executed?

(a) Break

(b) Continue

(c) 'this' keyword

(d) Static

Answer: (b)

(xvi) When there are multiple definitions with the same function name present in a class, what makes them different

(a) return type

(b) Number or types of arguments

(c) Name of arguments

(d) None of these

Answer: (b)

(xvii) If $z = 10$, find the value of M for the expression

$M = (5 * + + z) \% 4;$

(a) 4

(b) 3

(c) 1

(d) 2

Answer: (b)

(xviii) What should be the data type of 'k' the following code?

$k = (5 > 7)$? "true" ? "false";

(a) float

(b) String

(c) char

(d) Boolean

Answer: (b)

(xix) What is the return type of a java constructor?

(a) void

(b) int

(c) double

(d) No return type

Answer: (d)

(xx) What will be the output of the following statement?

System.out.println((Math.abs(-1)+Math.pow(2,3)));

(a) 7

(b) 10

(c) 9.0
(d) 18
Answer: (c)

Question 2.

(i) Give one example each of a primitive data type and a composite data type. **[2]**

(ii) Give one point of difference between unary and binary operators. **[2]**

(iii) Differentiate between call by value or pass by value and call by reference or pass by reference **[2]**

(iv) Write a Java expression for $\sqrt{2as + u^2}$ **[1]**

(v) Name the type of error (syntax, runtime, or logical error) in each case given below:
(a) Division by a variable that contains a value of zero. **[1]**
(b) Multiplication operator used when the operation should be division. **[1]**
(c) Missing semicolon. **[1]**

Question 3.

(i) If int $n[] = \{1, 2, 3, 5, 7, 9, 13, 16\}$ what are the values of x and y ? **[2]**
x = Math.pow(n[4], n[2]);
y = Math.sqrt(n[5] + [7]);

(ii) Write a statement each to perform the following task on a string: **[2]**
(a) Find and display the position of the last space in a string s.
(b) Convert a number stored in a string variable **x** to double data type.

(iii) What are the values of **x** and **y** when the following statements are executed? **[2]**
int a = 63, b = 36;
boolean $x = (a > b)$? true: false;
int $y = (a < b)? a: b$

(iv) State the values of **n** and**ch**. **[2]**
char c = ' A'.
int n = c + 1;
char ch = (char)n;

(v) What will be the result stored in **x** after evaluating the following expression? **[2]**
int x = 4; x+= $(x++) + (++x) + x$;

SECTION - B (40 Marks)

(Attempt any four questions from this section)

Question 4. **[15]**

Create a class **SpecialNumber** whose members are given below.

Data members: num (integer variable).

Methods:

(i) SpecialNumber(int p) :A parameterized constructor to assign value of p to num.

(ii) int factorial(int n) :Returns the factorial stored in n, when called.

(iii) void printArms( ) : Check and print that the number is Special number or not by calling factorial(int) function.

Write a main( ) method to create an object to call appropriate methods to print that a number is **Special** number or not.

EXAMPLE : 145 is a special number as 145 = $1!+4!+5!=145$

! is used for factorial. Factorial is the product of first N natural numbers.

Example: factorial of 4 or 4! = $1\times2\times3\times4=24$

[hint: Parameterized constructor will get the value at the time of object creation]

Question 5. **[15]**

Write a program to enter n Telephone numbers in a single dimension array and their owners in another array.. Search for a telephone number enter by the user. If number found then print the number along with owner name, otherwise print an appropriate message.

Question 6. **[15]**

Write a program to enter a number. Check and print that the number is a **Unique** number or not.

[A digit number will be unique if there are no repeated digits in the number]

EXAMPLE: 1324, 43, 54603 etc. are Unique numbers while 1321, 2302 etc are not.

Question 7. **[15]**

Write a program to print number of words along with words with consecutive aplhabets placed nextto each other.

Input Text : Abacus operates abstantially.

Output :

Number of Words : 4

Question 8. **[15]**

Write a program to enter two arrays of size 25, containing names of students in one array and their total marks (integer type) in second array. Arrange both arrays in descending order according to total marks. Print the merit list in the given format (**Use Bubble Sort**).

Merit List

Student Name Total marks

Question 9. **[15]**

Write a program to enter a string. Reprint the string so that each vowel is replaced by its next vowel.

Sample Input : It is an Umbrella

Sample Output : Ot Os en Ambrelle

ICSE 2023 EXAMINATION
SAMPLE PAPER- 2
COMPUTER APPLICATIONS

Maximum Marks: 100

Time allowed: Two hours

Answers to this Paper must be written on the paper provided separately.

You will not be allowed to write during the first 15 minutes.

This time is to be spent in reading the question paper.

The time given at the head of this Paper is the time allowed for-writing the answers: -

This Paper is divided into two Sections.

Attempt all questions from Section *A* and any four questions from Section *B*.

The intended marks for questions or parts of questions are given in brackets [].

SECTION - A (40 Marks)
(Attempt all question from this section)

Question 1.

Choose the correct answers to the questions from the given s. (Do not write the question, write the correct answer only.) **[20]**

(i) What is the return type of the **replace(char, char)** function:

(a) char

(b) boolean

(c) String

(d) Int

Answer: (c)

(ii) If int arr[ ] = {4,7,12, 8, 9, 10}; what is the value of p?

p = arr[arr.length – 1] + arr[0] * arr[1];

(a) 12

(b) 38

(c) 28

(d) 48

Answer (b)

(iii) Which keyword distinguishes between instance variable and class variable?

(a) class

(b) static

(c) this

(d) final

Answer: (b)

(iv) String s = "MISSISSIPPI";
System.out.println(s.indexOf('S')+s.lastIndexOf('s'));
(a) – 1
(b) 1
(c) 2
(d) – 2
Answer: (b)

(v) Element num[10] is which element of the array?
(a) 11th
(b) 9th
(c) 12th
(d) 8th
Answer: (a)

(vi) Visibility of ____________ variables are limited to the function, in which they are declared.
(a) Instance
(b) Arguments
(c) Class
(d) Local
Answer: (d)

(vii) compareTo( ) method returns:
(a) 1
(b) false
(c) int type value
(d) true
Answer: (c)

(viii) Which is the wrapper class for int data type?
(a) Int
(b) Integer
(c) integer
(d) None
Answer: (b)

(ix) Process of conversion from wrapper class to its respective primitive data type is called________
(a) Autoboxing
(b) Unboxing
(c) Encapsulation
(d) Method calling
Answer: (b)

(x) Block that always get executed no matter which kind of exception is thrown:

(a) finally( )

(b) default

(c) catch

(d) None

Answer: (a)

(xi) What is the return type of startsWith function?

(a) int

(b) boolean

(c) Boolean

(d) String

Answer: (b)

(xii) What is output of following?

char c = 'a';

short n = 26;

int m = c + n;

system.out.println (m);

(a) 2697

(b) 9726

(c) 123

(d) 112

Answer: (c)

(xiii) what should be value of 'k' in the following statement?

int k = 'a';

(a) a

(b) A

(c) 97

(d) 65

Answer: (c)

(xiv) In call by value __________ passes as arguments.

(a) Primitive data types

(b) Reference data types

Answer: (a)

(xv) for is a __________ statement in java.

(a) Iteration or looping

(b) branching

(c) decision making

(d) None of these

Answer: (a)

(xvi) What is the return type of IsLetterOrDigit function?

(a) int

(b) char

(c) boolean

(d) String

Answer: (c)

(xvii) Which value is printed by the following statement?

System.out.println(Math.rint(5.5));

(a) 5.0

(b) 5.5

(c) 6.0

(d) None of these

Answer: (c)

(xviii) Which of these is not a token?

(a) Operators

(b) Literals

(c) Identifiers

(d) Polymorphism

Answer: (d)

(xix) What will happen if you compile and executed the following code?

```
int i = 0;
for(i = 1 ; i <= 4 ; i++)
{continue;}
System.out.println(i);
```

(a) 0

(b) 4

(c) 5

(d) Compilation error

Answer: (c)

(xx) The list of variables present in the function call statement is known as

(a) Formal parameters

(b) Actual parameters

(c) Data members

(d) Array+•

Answer: (b)

Question 2.

(i) State the purpose and return data type of the following String functions:
(a) IndexOf().
(b) CompareTo(). **[2]**

(ii) What is the result stored in x, after evaluating the following expression int
Int $x = 5$; $x = x++ * 2 + 3 * --x$ **[2]**

(iii) Differentiate between static and non-static data members. **[2]**

(iv) Write the difference between length and length ( ) functions. **[2]**

(v) Differentiate between private and protected visibility modifiers. **[2]**

Question 3.

(i) State the values stored in the variables *strl* and *str*2 **[2]**
String $s1$ = "good"; String s2 = "world matters".
String str 1 = s2.substring(5). replace ('t', 'n');
String str 2 = s1.concat(str 1);

(ii) Rewrite the following program segment using the if...else statement. **[2]**
comm = (sale>> 15000)? sale* 5/100: 0

(iii) How many times will the following loop execute? What value will be returned? **[2]**
int $x = 2, y = 50$;
do{+ + x;$y = x + +$;} while (x <= 10);
return y;

(iv) What is the data type that the following library functions return? **[2]**
(a) isWhitespace (char ch)
(b) Math.random()

(v) Give the output of the following function when invoked **[2]**

```
void show()
{int y[ ] = {2, 4, 5, 8};
int q = y.length; int p = 0;for(int i = 0; i < q; i++){p=y[i] + y[3-i];
System.out.print(p+"\t");
   }
   }
```

SECTION - B (40 Marks)
(Attempt any four questions from this section)

Question 4. **[15]**

Define a class Employee having the following description:

Data members/Instance variables:

int pan	:	To store personal account number.
String name	:	To store name of employee.
double inc	:	To store annual taxable income.
double tax	:	to store tax that is calculated.

Member Function:

(i)	Employee()	:	Constructor to assign data members to their default values.
(ii)	void input()	:	To take input of pan, name and annual taxable income.
(iii)	void calcTax()	:	Calculate tax or an employee according to the following slab.
(iv)	void display()	:	Output details of an employee.

Write a main method() to compute the tax according to the given condition and display the output as per given format.

Taxable Annual Income	**Tax Rate**
Upto ` 1,00,000	No Tax
From `1,00,001 to `1,50,000	10% of the income exceeding `1,00,000
From `1,50,001 to `2,50,000	`5000 + 20% of the income exceeding `1,50,000
Above `2,50,000	`25,000 + 30% of the income exceeding `2,50,000

output:

Pan Number	**Name**	**Tax Income**	**Tax**
___	___	___	__

Question 5. **[15]**

Write a program to accept the names of 10 cities in a single dimension string array and their STD (Subscriber Trunk Dialing) codes in another single dimension integer array. Use **Linear** search method to search for a name of a city input by the user in the first list. If found display **Search Successful** and print the name of the city along with its STD code or else display the message **Search Unsuccessful**.

Question 6. **[15]**

Write a menu driven program to perform the following operations using switch case:

(a) Input a number and print that the number is Prime number or not.
[A number is said to be Prime, if it has only two factors. Example 2, 3, 5, etc]

(b) Input a number and print that the number is Perfect number or not.
[A number is said to be Perfect, if sum of all its factors (except the number) equals to number itself. Example: 6 is a perfect number as 1, 2, 3 and 6 are factors of 6 and 1 + 2 + 3 = 6]

Question 7. **[15]**

Write a program to initialize and array with the following numbers and sort them in descending order using Bubble sort technique. Print the sorted array.

21, 7, 12, 56, 32, 23, 45, 17, 22, 48

Question 8. **[15]**

Input a line of text from the user and create a new word formed out of the first letter of each word and convert the new word into uppercase.

Input: Mangoes are delivered after midday

Output: MADAM

Question 9. **[15]**

Design a class to overload a function printSeries( ) as follows:

(a) void printSeries(double x, int n): to compute and print the sum of the following serie

$$S = \frac{x}{2} - \frac{x^2}{4} + \frac{x^3}{6} - \frac{x^4}{8} + \ldots + \frac{x^n}{2n}$$

(b) void printSeries(String s):To print the string in the following format:

Example Input: ICSE

```
Output:  I
         I C
         I C S
         I C S E
```

Write a main method to create an object and invoke the above methods.

www.ingramcontent.com/pod-product-compliance
Ingram Content Group UK Ltd.
Pitfield, Milton Keynes, MK11 3LW, UK
UKHW061133310726
14090UKWH00037B/1287

9 789355 564924